PAPERS

of the

NEW WORLD ARCHAEOLOGICAL FOUNDATION

NUMBER EIGHTY-TWO

Chiapa de Corzo Montículo 32, su salvamento y consolidación

Chiapa De Corzo Mound 32, its salvage and consolidation

by

Eduardo Martínez Espinosa and Gareth W. Lowe

with contributions by

John E. Clark, Artemio Villatoro Alvarado, and Juan Carlos López Espinosa

VOLUME EDITOR

Mary E. Pye

New World Archaeological Foundation
Brigham Young University Press
Provo, Utah
2017

Chiapa de Corzo Montículo 32,

su salvamento y consolidación

Chiapa de Corzo, Mound 32,

its salvage and consolidation

Frontispicio: La Estructura G-1 del Montículo 32 de Chiapa de Corzo al término de su restauración en 1973. Bosquejo de José Nuñez Chanona, basado en una fotografía de *Historia de México*, Volume II (Navarrete 1978:302).

Frontispiece. Structure G-1 of Mound 32, Chiapa de Corzo, after its restoration in 1973. Sketch by José Nuñez Chanona based on a photograph in *Historia de México*, Volume II (Navarrete 1978:302).

ACKNOWLEDGMENTS

A book forty-five years in the making will inevitably not include everyone who should be acknowledged, but we attempt to do so as the authors would have done themselves. In 1972, the governor of the State of Chiapas, Dr. Manuel Velasco Suárez, signed the order for the salvage of Mound 32, provided funding, as well as access to heavy equipment. Such official state recognition likely reflects the combined cooperative efforts of the Instituto Nacional de Antropología e Historia (INAH) and the New World Archaeological Foundation (NWAF), personified in the two authors of this monograph: Ing. Eduardo Martínez Espinosa, then Delegate for Centro-INAH Chiapas, and Dr. Gareth Lowe, then Director of the NWAF. With the potential destruction of an important mound from the site of Chiapa de Corzo smack dab in the middle of the new bypass road to the modern town of Chiapa de Corzo, clearly there was an opportunity to involve political authorities and funding in saving cultural patrimony. With the uncovering of the largely intact Platform 32-G1, an even more tangible manifestation of cultural preservation was achieved.

Ing. Martínez oversaw the excavations at Md 32, utilizing workmen from the Office of Public Works under the direction of Ing. Rubén Valenti for the State of Chiapas. The NWAF also provided economic support with experienced technical field personnel, including Jorge Acuña N., Alejandro Sánchez G., Gilberto Utrilla, and night watchmen to guard the open excavations, as well as taking the lead on preliminary analysis and report preparation for the project. Critical institutional and professional support were given by Arqlgo. Eduardo Matos Moctezuma, then Sub-Director of the Department of Prehispanic Monuments of INAH, Arqlgo. Jorge Acosta, Arqlgo. César Sáenz, and Arquitecto Ignacio Marquina.

In recent times, detailed artifact description and analysis were undertaken by John E. Clark, Artemio Villatoro Alvarado, and Juan Carlos López Espinosa. Lynneth S. Lowe reviewed the text in Spanish. Translation of the text from Spanish into English was done by the volume editor, Mary E. Pye. Sandy Clark read the text. José Nuñez Chanona finalized several maps based on field sketches by Ing. Martínez. Students at Brigham Young University cleaned and enhanced the images that appear in this volume. Arlene Colman provided guidance for the student workers and undertook the critical and often complicated work of volume layout. Funding for the publication of this monograph was underwritten by the The David J. and Edloe Rust Memorial Fund, Department of Anthropology, Brigham Young University.

CONTENTS

FIGURES

CHIAPA DE CORZO MONTÍCULO 32,

SU SALVAMENTO Y CONSOLIDACIÓN

CHIAPA DE CORZO MOUND 32,

ITS SALVAGE AND CONSOLIDATION

Eduardo Martínez Espinosa y Gareth W. Lowe

INTRODUCCIÓN

Las investigaciones arqueológicas desarrolladas en el Montículo 32 del sitio arqueológico de Chiapa de Corzo, Chiapas, así como el presente informe, fueron el resultado de una fructífera cooperación entre el Instituto Nacional de Antropología e Historia (INAH), el Gobierno del Estado de Chiapas y la New World Archaeology Foundation (NWAF) de la Universidad Brigham Young. Antes de su desafortunado fallecimiento por accidente en 1988, el ingeniero Eduardo Martínez Espinosa había escrito lo siguiente:

Rescate de un Monumento Arqueológico: El Salvamento del Montículo 32 de Chiapa de Corzo

En el año de 1972, el Gobernador Constitucional del Estado de Chiapas, Dr. Manuel Velasco Suárez, tuvo a bien ordenar el rescate de la Estructura 32, la cual iba ser totalmente destruida al construirse la carretera de libramiento a la población de Chiapa de Corzo. Fue de gran fortuna que los restos arquitectónicos interiores de dicha estructura estuviesen casi en perfecto estado de conservación; al llevarse a cabo los trabajos de consolidación y restauración, éstos se basaron en lo estipulado en la Carta Internacional del Restauro o Carta de Venecia, quedando así protegido o restaurado un monumento prehispánico más (Frontispicio).

Las exploraciones del Montículo 32 tuvieron como objetivo primordial el salvamento arqueológico, con el fin de rescatarlo de la destrucción total motivada por la modernización, al ceder el paso a la urbanización de la ciudad. Al rescatar lo que se conserva in situ, se impide que siga destruyéndose, además de brindar una idea

INTRODUCTION

Archaeological investigations undertaken at Mound 32 of Chiapa de Corzo, Chiapas, as well as this report, were the result of a fruitful cooperation between the National Institute of Anthropology and History (INAH), the government of the state of Chiapas, and the New World Archaeological Foundation of Brigham Young University. Prior to his unfortunate passing in a car accident in 1988, Ing. Eduardo Martínez Espinosa had written the following:

Saving an Archaeological Monument: Salvage Work at Mound 32, Chiapa de Corzo

In 1972, the governor of the State of Chiapas, Dr. Manuel Velasco Suárez, had ordered the salvage of Structure 32, which was to be completely destroyed during construction of the highway to the town of Chiapa de Corzo. It was extremely fortunate that the interior architectural remains of this mound were in an almost perfect state of preservation; upon carrying out consolidation and restoration work, these remains, as stipulated in the Venice Charter for the Conservation and Restoration of Monuments and Sites,[1] would result in the protection and restoration of one more Prehispanic monument (see Frontispiece).

The primary objective of archaeological explorations at Mound 32 was to save it from total destruction caused by the modernization and urbanization of the

---

[1] Codification of international standards of conservation practices related to historic architecture; the charter was adopted in 1964 at the Second International Congress of Architects and Specialists of Historic Buildings.

más clara de cómo eran las estructuras y, ya consolidadas y reconstruidas, mostrar el grado de cultura alcanzado en la arquitectura prehispánica, que es mejor que mostrar solamente la pobreza de los montículos que queden sin explorar.

El Montículo 32 no fue más que uno de los 209 que existían hace más de 30 años, en que elaboré (en 1955) el plano topográfico de la Zona Arqueológica de Chiapa de Corzo (Figura 1), situada al este de la actual población; de esa época a la fecha han sido destruidos sin investigación más de 80 montículos. El estado general en que se encuentra la zona arqueológica actualmente es deplorable, pues la gente que vive en ella sigue utilizando los montículos para construir casas modernas, lo que produce la pérdida de información, ya que aún hay algunos montículos dignos de ser estudiados y conservados. La situación del Montículo 32 fue de la mayor importancia a este respecto, estando localizado directamente sobre la Carretera Panamericana. El Montículo 32 medía unos 6 m de altura y 50 m por lado, con un alargamiento bajo al oeste de 25 m. En la mayoría de los casos, los montículos en la zona arqueológica de Chiapa de Corzo presentan un estado avanzado de destrucción natural, debida al casi total abandono del sitio por muchos siglos, y el Montículo 32 era un ejemplo típico de ello (Figura 2). Sin embargo, casi al quitar las primeras piedras de la superficie durante la construcción de la carretera fueron apareciendo restos intactos de cuerpos arquitectónicos y de mampostería bien conservada. Para llevar a cabo un salvamento arqueológico del montículo, entonces, fui designado por el Arqlgo. Eduardo Matos Moctezuma, subjefe del Departamento de Monumentos Prehispánicos del INAH, fungiendo yo como Delegado del Centro INAH Chiapas en ese momento.

La mayor parte del financiamiento de los trabajos de salvamento arqueológico del Montículo 32 corrió a cargo del Gobierno del Estado de Chiapas, por lo cual hacemos

city. Preserving what remains in situ would impede continuing attempts to destroy it as well as provide a clearer idea as to what the structures looked like and, after consolidation and reconstruction, demonstrate the level of culture reached in Prehispanic architecture, which would be better than only showing the poor state of preservation of unexplored mounds.

Mound 32 was just one of 209 mounds that still existed more than 30 years ago, as shown in the 1955 topographic map of the Chiapa de Corzo Archaeological Zone (Figure 1), located east of the current town of the same name. Since that time more than 80 unexplored mounds have been destroyed. The current general state of the archaeological zone is deplorable, since people living nearby have been utilizing mound material to construct modern houses, resulting in a loss of information on mounds that deserve study and preservation. The situation of Mound 32 was key in this respect, being located directly in the line of the Pan-American Highway. Mound 32 measured some 6 m in height and 50 m on a side with a low western extension of some 25 m.

In the majority of cases, the mounds in the Chiapa de Corzo Archaeological Zone are in an advanced state of natural deterioration due to the almost complete abandonment of the site for many centuries; Mound 32 is a typical example of this (Figure 2). Nonetheless, almost upon removing the first stones from the surface during construction of the highway, the intact remains of architectural structures and well-preserved masonry appeared. I was designated by Arqlgo. Eduardo Matos Moctezuma, Sub-Director of the Department of Prehispanic Monuments of INAH, to carry out archaeological salvage operations at the mound while serving as Delegate of Centro-INAH Chiapas at that time.

The greater part of the financing for the archaeological salvage work at Mound 32 was paid for by the government of the State of Chiapas, for which we extend our

patente nuestro agradecimiento al entonces Gobernador de la entidad, Dr. Manuel Velasco Suárez, y al Ing. Rubén Valenti, Residente de la Secretaría de Obras Públicas en el Estado; al principio, los gastos de la excavación fueron costeados por esta secretaría. También agradecemos el aporte del arqueólogo Gareth W. Lowe y de la Fundación Arqueológica Nuevo Mundo (NWAF) por su ayuda económica y su colaboración, tanto en el campo como en el informe de los datos y en el análisis del material recuperado.

En el curso del salvamento, una vez encontrado algún indicio de construcción se precedió al desescombro y se dejó la evidencia in situ para su posterior consolidación y restauración, cuando ésta fuera posible, según lo ordenado por las autoridades del INAH, contándose con la asesoría personal de los arqueólogos Jorge Acosta, César Sáenz, Eduardo Matos y el arquitecto Ignacio Marquina. Como resultado, se ha restaurado ya totalmente una plataforma, utilizando las piedras talladas originales encontradas durante las excavaciones de los núcleos o rellenos de diferentes subestructuras, o aquéllas recuperadas de muros destruidos a causa de la obra de construcción de la carretera. Esperamos que los resultados hasta ahora obtenidos hagan ver a los patrocinadores y colaboradores que su esfuerzo ha valido la pena en el rescate de una importante zona arqueológica que es patrimonio cultural del Estado de Chiapas.

El informe que sigue fue preparado por Gareth Lowe, utilizando los informes, apuntes, fotografías y dibujos arquitectónicos del Ing. Martínez.

gratitude to then governor of the state, Dr. Manuel Velasco Suárez, and to Ing. Rubén Valenti, of the Office of Public Works of the state, whose office covered the excavation costs at the beginning of the project. We are also grateful to archaeologist Gareth W. Lowe and the New World Archaeological Foundation (NWAF) for their economic support and collaboration in the field, as well as with the report on the data and material analysis.

Over the course of the salvage project, once some indication of construction was encountered, we proceeded with the uncovering and left the evidence in situ for later consolidation and restoration whenever possible, as ordered by INAH authorities and with the advice of archaeologists Jorge Acosta, César Sáenz, Eduardo Matos, and the architect Ignacio Marquina. As a result, one platform has been completely restored using the original stones found during excavations of the mound interior, located in fills from various substructures, or recovered from walls destroyed by the highway construction work. We hope that the results to date obtained have demonstrated for the sponsors and collaborators that their efforts have validated the investment in the recovery of an important archaeological zone and cultural patrimony of the State of Chiapas.

The report that follows was prepared by Gareth Lowe, using various reports, notes, photographs, and architectural drawings by Ing. Martínez.

EL SALVAMENTO DEL MONTÍCULO 32

El proyecto original para la construcción de la carretera de libramiento de Chiapa de Corzo implicaba la destrucción total del Montículo 32, el cual ocupaba precisamente el punto de contacto con la Carretera Panamericana. Sin embargo, gracias a la rápida intervención de Eduardo Martínez Espinosa, entonces Delegado del INAH en Chiapas, se autorizó un plan de salvamento arqueológico urgente. Debido a la importancia de los edificios inmediatamente descubiertos se logró encontrar la manera de bifurcar la nueva carretera en la forma indicada en el plano (Figura 1), y fue posible rescatar una estructura interior del montículo y conservarla como monumento permanentemente accesible al público.

La Emergencia

Con el apoyo del Gobernador del Estado y de la Secretaría de Obras Públicas, el Ing. Martínez inició los trabajos de salvamento arqueológico del Montículo 32 de Chiapa el 28 de septiembre de 1972. Obras Públicas facilitó un equipo de 26 trabajadores con seis carretillas y la "ayuda" de maquinaria pesada para levantar escombros y quitar porciones de edificios que obstruían la nueva carretera. La NWAF, por su parte, proporcionó un ayudante técnico, Jorge Acuña N., un tractor-retroexcavadora, con su operador y técnico de larga experiencia, Alejandro Sánchez G., y vigilantes nocturnos. Se trabajó a marchas forzadas, con turnos de 12 horas diarias, hasta el 7 de noviembre, cuando se suspendió la ayuda que venía prestando el representante de la Secretaría de Obras Públicas. Se continuó entonces con la vigilancia de las dos tumbas, día y noche, por cuenta de la NWAF, hasta el día 14 del mismo mes en que fueron levantados los entierros y sus ofrendas de cerámica después de obtener los datos necesarios para su adecuada identificación y ubicación (ver Figuras 8-15). Más tarde, se renovó la ayuda por parte del gobierno para poder terminar la consolidación de la plataforma interior G1, a principios del año 1973.

Todo el trabajo de campo se realizó a través de la Delegación Chiapaneca del INAH, de la cual Eduardo Martínez Espinosa fungía

THE SALVAGE OF MOUND 32

The original project for the construction of the highway to Chiapa de Corzo implied the total destruction of Mound 32, which was located precisely at its crossroads with the Pan-American Highway. Thanks to the rapid intervention of Eduardo Martínez Espinosa, then Delegate of Centro-INAH in Chiapas, an emergency archaeological salvage project was authorized. Given the importance of the structures uncovered, a way to bifurcate the new highway was created as seen in the map (Figure 1), thereby making it possible to save the interior construction of the mound and preserve it permanently for public access.

The Emergency

With the support of the governor of the State of Chiapas and the Office of Public Works, Martínez began archaeological salvage work at Mound 32 of Chiapa de Corzo on September 28, 1972. The Public Works office provided a team of 26 workers with six wheelbarrows and the "help" of heavy machinery to remove the debris and cut those portions of the structures that were obstructing the new highway. The NWAF provided technician, Jorge Acuña N., backhoe operator, and long-time technician, Alejandro Sánchez G., and some night watchmen. The work progressed with 12-hour workdays until the 7th of November, when support was suspended by the Office of Public Works. The watchmen paid for by the NWAF continued guarding the two tombs, day and night, until the 14th of that same month when the burials and ceramic offerings were removed upon obtaining the necessary data for adequate identification and location of the artifacts (see Figures 8-15). Later, support was again provided by the government in early 1973 to complete the consolidation of the interior Platform G1.

All fieldwork was done by the Chiapas Delegation of INAH, under the charge of Eduardo Martínez Espinosa in those years.

Figura 1. Plano de la ubicación del Montículo 32 al interior del sitio arqueológico de Chiapa de Corzo, el cual muestra en gris el proyecto de la carretera de libramiento realizado en 1972. Se ilustra el sector occidental del sitio de Chiapa de Corzo según el levantamiento llevado a cabo por E. Martínez en 1955. El montículo adjunto, el 33, fue removido posteriormente para la construcción de una gasolinera; los Montículos 15 y 17 fueron destruidos posteriormente debido a las obras de edificación de la fábrica Nestlé.

Figure 1. Plan showing the location of Mound 32 in the middle of the archaeological site of Chiapa de Corzo; the shaded section shows the part of the highway project undertaken in 1972. The plan highlights the western sector of the site of Chiapa de Corzo according to a map made by Eduardo Martínez in 1955. The adjacent Mound 33 was removed prior to the construction of a gas station; Mounds 15 and 17 were subsequently destroyed by construction projects of the Nestlé Company.

como titular en aquellos años. El Ing. Martínez supervisó la obra en Chiapa de Corzo durante las mañanas, y tuvo a su cargo en particular el levantamiento de planos, los dibujos de plantas y cortes, la fotografía y la interpretación arquitectónica, además de la consolidación y restauración de los edificios conservados. La supervisión de trabajadores y albañiles fue labor de los encargados y técnicos de la NWAF, Jorge Acuña N., Alejandro Sánchez G. y Gilberto Utrilla.

En octubre de 1972 el gran muro y las esquinas de la Estructura G2 (ver Figuras 4-7, 11) fueron destruidos y removidos completamente por los tractores de la compañía constructora por estorbar a las labores de la carretera.[1] En tales casos, cuando el trabajo de la construcción de la carretera no podía esperar para poder descubrir íntegramente todas las secciones de las subestructuras originales hubo que limitarse a rescatar información gráfica, y a veces únicamente fotográfica. Sin embargo, por estar presentes en la obra, y con el esfuerzo y apoyo de varios oficiales locales, sí se pudo explorar totalmente otra subestructura más temprana que, por buena fortuna, quedó descubierta por la obra de los tractores; ésa es la Estructura 32-G1 que se describirá más adelante.

Debido al presupuesto limitado que se asignó para el rescate del Montículo 32, se pensaban descubrir, con suerte, solamente porciones de una estructura o estructuras que se lograsen rescatar, esperando poder reconstruir alguna entidad inteligible. La suerte de encontrar la Plataforma 32-G1 hizo posible la restauración de una subestructura completa sin mayores gastos. La Estructura 32-G1 (así llamada por ser el primer edificio —a nuestro saber— de la fase Guanacaste o Chiapa V en el lugar) conservaba su altura original de cerca de 2.50 m y en su superficie quedaban todavía una serie de plataformas secundarias y, encima de ellas, los restos de un templo con tres cuartos.

Martínez oversaw the work at Chiapa de Corzo in the mornings. His particular responsibility was developing maps, drawings of the floors and stratigraphic cuts, photography, and architectural interpretation, in addition to the consolidation and restoration of the surviving structures. The workmen and masons were supervised by NWAF technicians, Jorge Acuña N., Alejandro Sánchez G., and Gilberto Utrilla.

In October of 1972, the great wall and the corners of Structure G2 (see Figures 4-7) were destroyed and completely removed by tractors by the construction company because they were obstructing work on the highway.[1] In such cases, when the highway construction work could not wait for the complete uncovering of all sections of the original substructures, the crew was limited to recovering graphic information, and at times only photographs. Still, by being present during the highway construction, and with the support and efforts of various local officials, the crew could explore completely the earliest substructure, which, by good fortune, had been discovered by road crew tractors; this was Structure 32-G1 and will be described further below.

Given the limited budget assigned for the Mound 32 Salvage Project, it was thought that only, with luck, certain portions of a structure or structures would be recovered, with the hope it would be sufficient to reconstruct something intelligible. The fortuitous finding of Platform 32-G1 allowed for the restoration of an entire substructure without great cost. Structure 32-G1 (so-called for being the first structure—to our knowledge—of the Guanacaste or Chiapa V phase) still stood at its original height of 2.5 m and its surface still held a series of secondary platforms and, on top of these, the remains of

---

[2] Este sistema de numeración de edificios es al revés de la tradicional para Chiapa de Corzo. Martínez y Lowe dan el número 1 al edificio más antiguo de la fase, pero en su trabjo anterior, el número 1 fue el primer edificio econtrado en excavación de una fasé, o sea, el último o más reciente y no al primero (véa Lowe 1960:4, 6).

This numbering system for buildings is the reverse of the traditional way of designating buildings for Chiapa de Corzo. Martínez and Lowe designate as Number 1 the earliest building of a phase, but in earlier work Number 1 was reserved for the first building of a phase found in excavation, or in other words, the most recent rather than the earliest (see Lowe 1960:4, 6).

Por cierto, no sabemos si existe o no otra plataforma más antigua debajo de G1; ningún esfuerzo fue hecho en aquel momento para investigar el interior de la plataforma por falta de tiempo, presupuesto y autorización. No obstante, quedamos satisfechos con el salvamento de una secuencia arquitectónica muy importante y la restauración de una subestructura completa correspondiente al periodo Preclásico Tardío, con una preservación casi única en México.

El Rescate

Después de limpiar totalmente la superficie del Montículo 32 (Figura 2) se procedió a colocar una estacada en retícula cada cinco metros. Iniciamos las exploraciones por medio de dos calas de aproximación hacia la estructura, con el plan de continuar tierra adentro hasta encontrar la base o bases de algún muro o piso. Mediante la cala del lado sur del montículo (Figura 3a) se procedió a excavar unidades de 2 m por lado; se encontró luego la base en talud de un primer cuerpo y parte de los tres primeros escalones de un escalera central (ver Figura 26); todo ello indicaba que aquí se hallaba el frente de la plataforma o de una serie de plataformas enterradas.

Las excavaciones en el lado poniente del Montículo 32 rápidamente revelaron una situación más complicada (Figuras 3b, 5 y 6). Por necesidades de la nueva carretera, los constructores al principio desmontaron con tractor la mayor parte de una plataforma baja ubicada en el lado oeste del Montículo 32, una acción que dejó a la vista evidencias de los arranques de muros en talud. Después de limpiar el relleno existente detrás de tales cimientos, se encontró entonces un tercer muro o talud de mampostería, éste intacto, con una altura mayor a dos metros (correspondiente a la Estructura G2; ver Figura 3b, y el plano en la Figura 4). Encima de esta plataforma alta se encontró un piso muy quebrado, lo cual no permitió entender bien la forma original de su orilla. Una escalera angosta se encontraba remetida en el muro, y permitía el acceso a la superficie de la estructura por el lado occidental (Figura 5).

El talud G2 resultó ser bastante impresionante cuando fue liberado en toda su extensión norte-sur (Figuras 6, 12 y 19). A pesar

a temple with three rooms. We do not know whether another, older platform exists under G1; no effort was made at that moment to investigate the interior of the platform for lack of time, budget, and authorization. Nonetheless, we were satisfied with salvaging a very important architectural sequence and restoring a complete Late Preclassic substructure—a preservation almost unique in Mexico.

The Salvage Project

After cleaning the Mound 32 surface (Figure 2), the crew proceeded to place stakes in a grid pattern every five meters. We began the explorations with two trenches from the edge of the structure towards the interior with the idea of continuing them until the base(s) of a wall or floor were hit. By means of a trench on the south side of the mound (Figure 3a,) we excavated units of 2 m on a side. We found the base of a sloping wall of the first structure and part of the first three stairs of a central stairway (Figure 26); all of which indicated that we had found the front of the platform or a series of buried platforms.

Excavations on the east side of Mound 32 rapidly revealed a more complicated situation (Figures 3b, 5-6). For the new road, workmen using a tractor had stripped away most of a low platform on the west side of Mound 32, an action that left visible evidence of the bases of two sloping walls. After cleaning the fill behind these wall bases, we found a third sloping masonry wall, this one intact, with a height greater than 2 m (corresponding to Structure G2; see Figure 3b, and the plan in Figure 4). On top of this high platform a broken-up floor was found. We did not find its original edges. A narrow stairway was located inset into the wall that permitted access to the surface of the structure on the west side (Figure 5).

The G2 exterior wall was fairly impressive in its north-south extension when completely uncovered (Figures 6, 12, 19). In spite of its

a.

b.

Figura 2. Vistas del Montículo 32 al inicio de las excavaciones en octubre de 1972. a. vista al norte desde la Carretera Panamericana. b. esquina noreste del montículo cortado por la nueva carretera de libramiento; la Carretera Panamericana se encuentra al centro y al extremo izquierdo de la fotografía y la fábrica Nestlé se ve al fondo.

Figure 2. Views of Mound 32 at the beginning of excavations in October of 1972; a. looking north from the Pan-American Highway; b. northeast corner of the mound cut by the new highway; the Pan-American Highway can be seen at center-left of the photograph and a Nestlé building appears in the background.

Figura 3. Inicio de las excavaciones en el Montículo 32. a. vista al noreste, que se muestra los accesos al frente y al occidente del montículo. b. restos de construcciones encontrados en las capas exteriores del montículo, con la muralla G-4 arriba y la Plataforma G-2 abajo.

Figure 3. Beginning of excavations at Mound 32; a. view to the northeast showing accesses on the front and west sides of the mounds; b. remains of walls found in the outer layers of the mound, with wall G-4 above and Platform G-2 below.

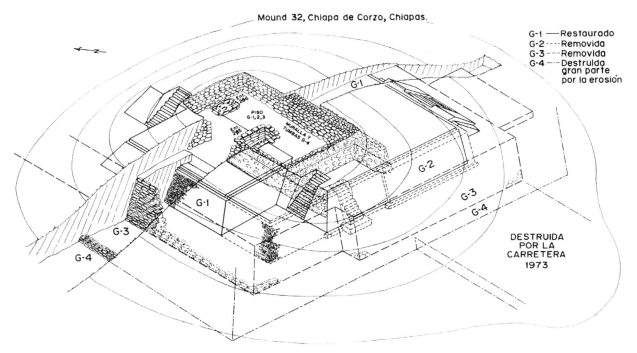

Figura 4. Secuencia de construcciones en el Montículo 32. Dibujo de José Nuñez Chanona basado en un borrador preparado por E. Martínez. Las Plataformas G-2, G-3 y G-4 fueron destruidas por la carretera y removidas durante las excavaciones.

Figure 4. Construction sequence of Mound 32. Drawing by José Nuñez Chanona based on a draft prepared by Eduardo Martínez. Platforms G-2, G-3, and G-4 were destroyed by highway construction and removed during excavations.

Figura 5. Vista del centro de la Plataforma G-2 y la gran muralla G-4 del "patio hundido" superpuesta encima de ella. Al este, se aprecia al Ing. Martínez parado a la izquierda. El tripié con alidada está encima de la tumba del Entierro 87.

Figure 5. View of the center of Platform G-2 and great wall G-4 of the "sunken patio" superimposed over them. Ing. Martínez is standing to the east. The tripod and alidade are located on top of the tomb of Burial 87.

Figura 6. Vista general de la Plataforma G-2 y la muralla y "patio" interior G-4 arriba de ella (lado occidental completamente descubierto).

Figure 6. General view of Platform G-2 and the wall and interior "patio" G-4 above it (western side completely uncovered).

Figura 7. Liberación parcial de la superficie de la Plataforma G-1 con la muralla interior de G-4 superpuesta encima; la tapa de la tumba del Entierro 87 ha aparecido en el centro (faltaba aún por retirar el relleno, visible delante de las personas de pie, Gareth Lowe y Alejandro Sánchez).

Figure 7. Partial clearing of the surface of Platform G-1 with the interior wall G-4 above it; the covering over the Burial 87 tomb appears in the center (not yet removed from the fill, visible in front of Gareth Lowe and Alejandro Sánchez).

de su magnífico aspecto y su buen estado de conservación, el muro G2 fue destruido casi inmediatamente después de su descubrimiento por los tractores de la compañía constructora de caminos. Afortunadamente, fue posible aprovechar esta destrucción para limpiar una subestructura más antigua y aún más completa, casi igualmente bien conservada, la Estructura G1, como se ha explicado anteriormente. Para más detalles, ver la siguiente sección dedicada a la consolidación y restauración del edificio (compárense las Figuras 4, 17 y 34).

De igual o mayor importancia para la historia antigua de Chiapa de Corzo, apareció un gran "patio hundido" encima de la Subestructura G2, construido con muros de piedra bola que

magnificent appearance and good state of preservation, this wall was destroyed almost immediately after its discovery by tractors from the road construction company. Fortunately, it was possible to take advantage of this destruction to uncover an older and even more complete substructure, almost equally well preserved, Structure G1, as explained previously. For more details, see the following section on the consolidation and restoration of the structure (compare Figures 4, 17, and 34).

Of equal or greater importance for the ancient history of Chiapa de Corzo, a large "sunken patio" appeared on top of Substructure G2, constructed with walls of river cobbles,

alcanzaban los 2 m de altura (Figuras 3-9). Estos muros de contención sobrepasaban la altura de los taludes de las Subestructuras G1, G2 y, aparentemente, G3; es decir, esta construcción de tipo provisional conservó abierto por un tiempo desconocido un espacio o "patio" bastante extenso, hundido en la superficie de una ampliación muy grande a la plataforma G2 (y probablemente a la G3 también). Dicha ampliación la podemos relacionar con la Estructura G4, cuyos muros exteriores quedaron casi destruidos por el saqueo y la erosión natural del montículo a lo largo de los siglos. Este "patio hundido", de aspecto provisional, nos recordó inmediatamente a otra situación idéntica encontrada en el Montículo 1 (ver Discusión), en cuyo caso se pudo inferir que los antiguos pobladores de Chiapa esperaban enterrar algún personaje o funcionario de importancia antes de finalizar una ampliación mayor a la plataforma más grande de la comunidad. Resultaba entonces casi seguro que aquí, en el Montículo 32, también se hubiese colocado un entierro de otro funcionario de alto rango; previsiblemente debería haber alguna clase de tumba colocada en el fondo de tal "patio hundido".

La limpieza completa del "patio hundido" confirmó la situación esperada: la presencia de dos tumbas intrusivas en el piso superior de la Plataforma G1 (Figuras 6-9). La gran muralla de contención de piedra bola claramente rodeaba el espacio amplio y vacío, dejado abierto durante la construcción, en donde se esperaba colocar la sepultura, correspondiente al Entierro 87. Solamente al continuar con el proceso de relleno del patio fue enterrado otro individuo, el Entierro 88, probablemente en calidad de acompañante. Después de ocupar las tumbas, la Plataforma 32 completó su nueva edificación. Todas las subestructuras anteriores quedaron enterradas por debajo de cuando menos 2 m de aumento vertical al terminarse la Estructura G4, y se incrementó también la extensión horizontal en varios metros, al parecer, en todas las direcciones.

Por la severidad de la erosión natural sufrida durante veinte siglos, no es posible conocer ni el tamaño preciso ni el carácter arquitectónico de la Plataforma G4. Es probable, sin embargo, por lo que sabemos

that reached 2 m in height (Figures 3-9). These retaining walls exceeded the height of the exterior walls of Substructures G1, G2, and, apparently, G3. That is to say, this provisional construction preserved for an unknown amount of time an open space or "patio" sunk into the surface of a very large structural extension to Platform G2 (and probably to G3 as well). This extension can be tied to Structure G4, the walls of which were almost destroyed by looting and erosion of the mound over the centuries. This temporary "sunken patio" immediately reminded us of an identical situation encountered at Mound 1 (see Discussion section), which we interpreted as evidence that the ancient inhabitants of Chiapa de Corzo held off from interring some significant elite individual so as to finish the large extension to the largest platform of the community. And so it seemed certain here at Mound 32 that another individual of high status would have been placed in a tomb below the sunken patio.

Clearing out the "sunken patio" area confirmed the expected: the presence of two intrusive tombs in the upper floor of Platform G1 (Figures 6-9). The large retaining wall of stone cobbles clearly surrounded the wide empty space, leaving it open during construction while awaiting the placement of the tomb, Burial 87. In the process of backfilling the patio, another individual was buried, Burial 88, probably to accompany the individual in Burial 87. After placing the occupants and offerings in the tombs, construction was completed in this area of Platform 32. All of the previous substructures were then buried under 2 m of vertical fill placed to complete Structure G4. It seems there was also added some meters of horizontal extension in all directions.

The degree of natural erosion that has occurred over twenty centuries renders it impossible to know the precise size or architectural character of Platform G4. It is probable, however, given what we know of other

de otras situaciones en Chiapa de Corzo que la G4 mantuviese mayormente el estilo de la Plataforma G1, pero a una escala mucho mayor, es decir, con el doble de altura, y un mayor ancho y largo. Sin duda, se mantuvo hasta la planta arquitectónica básica en forma de "T", con la parte posterior más angosta, que sostenía a su vez un templo sencillo. Sabemos, por supuesto, que las plataformas con mayor superficie generalmente incluían un patio con edificios a los tres lados, mientras que el frente quedaba abierto, pero en el caso de la Estructura 32-G4 nada quedaba de su superficie para indicar algo concreto sobre tal posibilidad. Más detalles de la arquitectura del Montículo 32 se incluyen en la sección de Consolidación y Restauración.

ENTIERROS Y SUS OFRENDAS

[*Nota editorial: La numeración de los entierros excavados en Chiapa de Corzo siguió un número de la lista maestra para todos los entierros en el sito. Un resumen reciente de la lista maestra de entierros encontró algunas repeticiones, en específico para los números 295 y 296. Los números de entierros en el Montículo 32 fueron cambiados para corregir la lista maestra; por lo tanto, las fotos de campo y las subsecuentes fotos de los artefactos presentan números diferentes de los del texto; en particular, el Entierro 295 se convirtió en el Entierro 87/Tumba 12 y el Entierro 296 se convirtió en el Entierro 88/Tumba 13.*]

Durante las investigaciones del Montículo 32 se encontraron tres entierros, dos de ellos ubicados en las tumbas del "patio hundido" antes mencionadas y el otro al pie de la escalera lateral de la Estructura G2. Según la cerámica depositada como parte las ofrendas funerarias, los tres entierros corresponden a la fase Guanacaste o Chiapa V del periodo Preclásico Tardío, que puede fecharse alrededor de un siglo o dos antes de la era actual.

Entierro 87/ Tumba 12 (Figuras 8-11)

Edad y sexo: Adulto maduro, según su estatura y dentadura; la mala condición de los huesos (Figura 10) no permitió observaciones del sexo, aunque por su robustez se puede suponer que era

instances at Chiapa de Corzo, that Platform G4 generally maintained the same style as G1 but at a much larger scale—in other words, double the height and much wider. Undoubtedly, it maintained its "T-shaped" architectural ground plan with a narrower upper section that supported a simple temple structure. We know, of course, that platforms with larger surface areas typically included a plaza with buildings on three side, while the front remained open. In the case of Structure 32-G4, unfortunately, nothing remained on the surface to indicate that such had been the case. More details on the architecture of Mound 32 will be included in the Consolidation and Restoration section.

BURIALS AND OFFERINGS

[*Editorial note: Burial numbers at Chiapa de Corzo were assigned from a master burial list for all burials at the site. Recent review of the master burial list found some duplications, specifically for burial numbers 295 and 296. The burial numbers for Mound 32 were therefore changed to avoid duplication of numbers. Hence, field and artifact photographs present different numbers from those in the text. Burial 295 became Burial 87/Tomb 12 and Burial 296 became Burial 88/Tomb 13.*]

During the Mound 32 investigations, three burials were uncovered. Two were located in the tombs of the "sunken patio" as previously mentioned, and the other was found at the foot of the side stairway of Structure G2. According to the ceramics deposited as funerary offerings, the three burials date to the Guanacaste or Chiapa V phase of the Late Preclassic period, which can be dated to around one or two centuries before the Common Era.

Burial 87/ Tomb 12 (Figures 8-11)

Age and Sex: Mature adult, according to stature and dentition; the poor condition of the bones (Figure 10) did not allow typing as to sex, although their robustness could lead

a.

b.

Figura 8. La gran muralla interior G-4 y las tumbas. a. mirando al este, atrás del "patio hundido" dejado en el relleno de la ampliación para la Plataforma G-4, con la Tumba 12/ Entierro 87 en el centro y la Tumba 13/ Entierro 88 al fondo; b. el mismo "patio hundido" mirando al occidente con la Tumba 12/ Entierro 87 en medio.

Figure 8. The great interior wall G-4 and the tombs; a. looking east, behind the "sunken patio" in the fill of the Platform G-4 extension; Tomb 12/ Burial 87 is in the center and Tomb 13/ Burial 88 in the background; b. the same "sunken patio" looking to the west with Tomb 12/ Burial 87 in the middle.

Figura 9. Cubierta de la tumba del Entierro 87, intrusiva en la Plataforma G-1. a: lajas que tapaban la tumba, vistas desde el sur y el norte (foto b); c-d: incensario de plato con tres picos y su vasija de soporte colocada debajo de una laja de la tapa (vea Figure 10).

Figure 9. Covering over the tomb of Burial 87; burial was intruded into Platform G-1; a. stone slabs covering the tomb, seen from the south and to the north (photo b); c-d. three-horned censer plate and the vessel supporting it found under a stone slab of the tomb covering (see Figure 10).

Figura 10. Tumba y restos óseos del Entierro 87.

Figure 10. Tomb and skeletal remains of Burial 87.

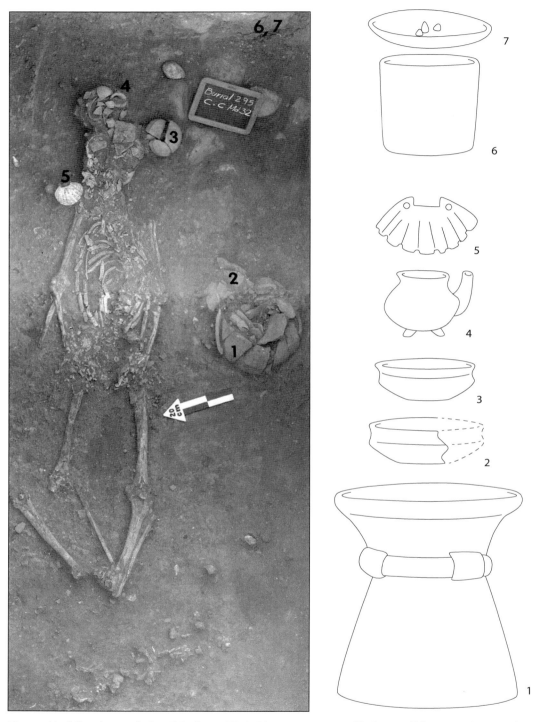

Figura 11. Ofrenda asociada al Entierro 87. 1. Florero o urna, café claro pulido; 2, 3. Platos cafetosos burdos; 4. Ollita color crema; 5. Concha marina, color anaranjado, trabajada, originalmente cubría la boca, sin duda; 6, 7. Incensario de plato con tres picos y un hueco en el fondo, con su vasija de base, cerámica café burdo.

Figure 11. Offering associated with Burial 87: 1. Florero or urn, polished light brown slip; 2-3. Coarse brown bowls; 4. Small cream-colored jar; 5. Marine shell, orange and worked, undoubtedly originally covered the mouth; 6-7. Three-horned censer plate with a hole in the base and its supporting vessel, coarse brown.

masculino (el esqueleto in situ midió 1.76-1.80 m de la cima del cráneo a la zona de los talones, medida indicativa de una persona de buen tamaño). De éste y del Entierro 88, Eduardo Martínez anotó lo siguiente: "De los esqueletos únicamente se trasladaron los cráneos, en pedazos, para su estudio más cuidadoso, lo restante de la osamenta por su estado de descomposición no es posible preservarlo con los medios con que se cuentan."

Posición: Extendido, dorsal, con la cabeza al sureste, manos sobre la cintura o pelvis. Las falanges fueron separadas de las tibia, tal vez movidos por animales, y la tibia derecha estaba algo fuera de su lugar, probablemente por una laja caída del techo.

Sepultura: Cámara o tumba excavada en el relleno de la Plataforma 32-G1 a una profundidad aproximada de 1 m, con techo de lajas delgadas de piedra colocadas al nivel del piso de la plataforma y sin duda sostenidas por vigas de madera. Según el dibujo de Martínez (Figura 4), las paredes de la tumba eran de bloques de piedra o de ladrillos de adobe (comunes en el Montículo 1), pero no hay datos al respeto.

Ofrenda (Figura 11):

1. Florero o urna grande colocada a un lado del cuerpo y encontrada completamente fragmentada. Había sido cubierta originalmente con una capa de estuco delgado o de pigmento color rojo, ya todo caído;

2, 3. Platos burdos de silueta compuesta, uno hallado cerca a la cabeza y el otro probablemente cubriéndola;

4. Ollita pequeña con vertedera y soportes sub-cónicos y sólidos, colocada junto a la cabeza;

5. Concha marina, al parecer Spondyllus trabajada para remover las espinas, cortada y perforada para suspensión; probablemente fue puesta sobre la boca del difunto. El color es rojizo con amarillo.

6. Vasija profunda de paredes verticales, enterrada boca arriba debajo de una laja del techo; sostenía el No. 7 y parece haber funcionado como base para un brasero.

one to suppose he was male (the skeleton in situ measured 1.76-1.80 m from the top of the cranium to the area of the heels, a measurement indicating a good-sized individual). For this individual and the one from Burial 88, Eduardo Martínez noted the following: "Of the skeletal remains encountered, only the crania were removed, in pieces, for more careful study. Because of its state of decomposition we could not preserve it with the means we had at hand."

Position: Extended, lying face up, with head facing to the southeast, hands over the waist or pelvis. The phalanges were separated from the tibiae, perhaps moved by animals, and the right tibia was also out of place, probably caused by a fallen slab from the tomb cover.

Grave type: Chamber or excavated tomb in the fill of Platform 32-G1 at a depth of 1 m, with a covering of thin stone slabs located at the level of the floor of the platform and undoubtedly supported by wooden beams. According to the drawing by Martínez (Figure 4), the walls of the tomb were stone blocks or adobe bricks (common at Mound 1), but there is no further information.

Offering (Figure 11):

1. Florero or large urn, complete but in fragments, located to one side of the body. Originally it had been covered by a thin layer of stucco or red pigment, now fallen away.

2, 3. Coarse bowls with composite silhouette walls, one found near the head and the other probably covering it.

4. Small jar with a spout and solid sub-conical supports, located next to the head.

5. Marine shell, probably worked Spondyllus, with spines removed, cut, and perforated to be suspended; probably located over the mouth of the deceased. The color is yellowish red.

6. Deep cylinder with straight walls, buried upright. Vessel 7 rested on top of it and seems to have functioned as the base for the censer. Both were under a slab from the roof of the tomb.

Figura 12. Plataformas G-2, G-3, G-4 y tumba del Entierro 88. Arriba: vista general desde el sur de la Plataforma G-2 con la carretera nueva a la derecha; a la izquierda se ve el resto de un muro exterior de la Plataforma G-3; Abajo: lajas que cubrían el Entierro 88 en el "patio hundido" dejado en el interior del aumento G-4. Debido a la construcción de la carretera fue necesario destruir la Plataforma G-2.

Figure 12. Platforms G-2, G-3, G-4 and tomb of Burial 88. Above: general view from the south side of Platform G-2 with the new highway to the right; to the left one can see the remains of an exterior wall from Platform G-3. Below: stone slabs that covered Burial 88 in the "sunken patio" left during the construction of the G-4 extension. Due to the highway construction, it was necessary to destroy and remove Platform G-2.

Figura 13. Tumba, restos óseos y ofrenda del Entierro 88. La tumba y el Entierro 88 mirando al oeste.
Figure 13. Tomb, skeletal remains, and offerings of Burial 88. The tomb and Burial 88 looking west.

Figura 14. Acercamiento del cráneo, torso y ofrenda.
Figure 14. Close-up of skull, torso, and offerings.

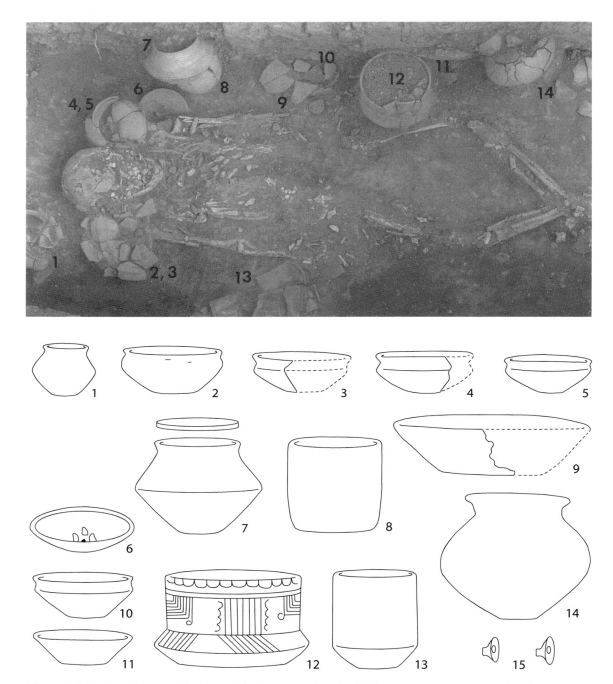

Figura 15. Entierro 88 y su ofrenda. 1. Vasija crema; 2-5, 8-11: Platos y vaso con tapa, todos de cerámica cafetosa burda; 6. Brasero con tres picos, café burdo; 7. Olla de cerámica "Mirador Anaranjado Vítreo"; 15: orejeras de piedra verde.

Figure 15. Burial 88 and offering: 1. Cream-colored vessel; 2-5, 8-11. Bowls and a vase with a cover, all coarse brownware; 6. Three-horned censer plate, coarse brown; 7. Mirador Vitreous Orange jar; 15. Greenstone ear flares.

7. Plato-brasero con tres pequeños picos o cuernos y una perforación en el fondo; fue colocado encima de un recipiente, la vasija No. 6 (Figura 9d);

8. Dos cuentas, una de jadeíta (8 mm) y otra de barro, cilíndrica (1 cm de largo).

Entierro 88/ Tumba 13 (Figuras 12-15)

Edad y sexo: Juvenil, sexo desconocido; esqueleto completamente fragmentado (ver comentario al Entierro 87).

Posición: Extendido, dorsal, con la cabeza al noroeste, brazos al lado del cuerpo y rodillas abiertas con los tobillos encimados o cruzados.

Sepultura: Excavada a poca profundidad en la superficie de la Plataforma 32-G1, 3 m al nororiente del Entierro 87; la tumba había sido repellada con barro y tapada con lajas de piedra sobre vigas de madera ya desaparecidas. La tapa quedaba más arriba de la superficie o piso de la plataforma G1 (al interior del "patio hundido" de G4), y la tumba daba el aspecto de haber sido introducida desde arriba entre un relleno ya existente sobre el piso (ver Figura 8a).

Ofrenda (Figura 15):

1. Ollita rojiza con ligeras acanaladuras;

2-5. Dos pares de platos burdos de color café, colocados un par a cada lado de la cabeza;

6. Plato-brasero con tres pequeños picos y una perforación en el fondo, puesto sobre el piso junto al hombro izquierdo;

7. Olla de cerámica tipo Mirador Anaranjado Vítreo, colocado encima del vaso No. 8; cuya tapa era un disco de cerámica bien elaborado a partir de un tiesto grande;

8. Vaso color café vertical.

9-11. Platos burdos color café, aplastados, colocados junto al brazo izquierdo; uno puesto abajo, contenía restos de pigmento rojo;

12. Vasija de boca ancha, paredes rectas y base bulbosa con fondo plano; negra pulida con diseños geométricos incisos en el exterior;

13. Vaso angosto, de color gris cremoso, aplastado;

7. Plate-censer with three small, inner points or horns and a perforation in the center; it was located under Vessel 6 (Figure 9d).

8. Two beads, one of jadeite (8 mm) and the other of clay, cylindrical (1 cm in length).

Burial 88/ Tomb 13 (Figures 12-15)

Age and sex: Juvenile, sex unknown; skeleton completely fragmented (see commentary for Burial 87).

Position: Extended, lying face up, with head to the northeast, arms at the sides and knees open with the ankles crossed.

Grave type: Excavated slightly below the surface of Platform 32-G1, 3 m to the northeast of Burial 87; the tomb had been plastered over with clay and sealed with stone slabs over wooden beams, which have decomposed. The covering was located above the surface or floor of Platform G1 (the interior of the sunken patio of G4), and the tomb appeared to have been inserted from above into fill already present on the floor (see Figure 8a).

Offerings (Figure 15):

1. Reddish small jar with shallow grooves.

2-5. Two pairs of coarse brown bowls, one pair located on each side of the head.

6. Plate-censer with three small, inner horns and a perforation in the center, located on the floor next to the left shoulder.

7. Mirador Vitreous Orange jar, with z-angle walls, located on top of Vessel 8, and a disc-shaped ceramic cover, well made from a large sherd.

8. Brown cylinder with vertical walls.

9-11. Coarse brown bowls, flattened, located next to the left arm; one placed downward with red pigment remains.

12. Deep bowl with wide mouth, straight walls, and a bulbous base; polished black slip with geometric designs incised on the exterior.

13. Narrow cylinder, creamy gray color, flattened.

14. Olla anaranjada;

15. Par de orejeras pequeñas de piedra verde pulida, una a cada lado del cráneo;

16. Grupo de 11 piedritas de cuarzo blanco (parece ser una sola piedra del río quebrada) colocado sobre el vientre; probablemente fueron contenidas en un bolsa.

Entierro 297 (Figura 16)

Edad y sexo: Infantil, sexo desconocido por quedar pocos fragmentos de hueso.

Posición: Probablemente sedente.

Sepultura: Fosa angosta y simple, excavada en un relleno de tierra y piedra, con el cuerpo y la ofrenda colocados desde arriba, encimándose, y después cubiertos con unas lajas.

Ofrenda (Figura 16):

1. Platón grande de fondo plano y borde ancho volteado y acanalado, de color rojo pulido;

2-4, 8-10. Ollita y platos con baño café-negruzco bien pulido; el No. 4 es de perfil compuesto con una serie de triángulos rayados esgrafiados sobre el cuello;

5-7. Plato y ollitas de cerámica cremosa pulida, con manchas o bordes pintados en rojo;

11. Plato ahumado negruzco y pulido con leve restos de un diseño negativo de rayas paralelos; probablemente tipo Usulután e importado del sur (América Central).

CONSOLIDACIÓN Y RESTAURACIÓN DE LA ESTRUCTURA 32-G1

Las labores de salvamento de emergencia llevadas a cabo en el Montículo 32, descritas en la sección anterior, nos habían aportado los restos aislados de una sola subestructura bastante antigua y casi intacta; esta plataforma la identificamos como 32-G1 (Figura 17). Para librar dicha plataforma había que quitar la mitad de la altura del Montículo 32 y también eliminar casi la mitad de su extensión horizontal.

El descubrimiento total de la Estructura 32-G1 fue logrado a través de muchos esfuerzos por parte de los trabajadores y supervisores;

14. Orange jar.

15. Pair of small greenstone ear flares, one on each side of the skull.

16. Group of 11 small white quartz stones (appears to be a single broken river stone) located on the abdomen, probably once in a bag.

Burial 297 (Figure 16)

Age and sex: Infant, sex unknown, only a few bone fragments remaining.

Position: Probably seated.

Grave Type: Simple, narrow pit, excavated into earth and stone fill, with the body and then offerings interred from above, with stone slabs placed over it.

Offerings (Figure 16):

1. Large, shallow, flat-bottom bowl with wide-everted, grooved rim and polished red slip.

2.-4, 8-10. Bowls with polished black-brown slip. Vessels 4, 8 and 10 have composite silhouette forms; Vessel 4 also has a series of striped triangles incised on the shoulder.

5-7. Bowl and small jars with polished, creamy white slip and painted red rims.

11. Flat-bottomed bowl with medial flange, polished smoky black with traces of parallel lines in negative resist; probably Usulután and imported from the south (Central America).

CONSOLIDATION AND RESTORATION OF STRUCTURE 32-G1

The emergency salvage work carried out at Mound 32, described in the previous section, has provided us with the isolated remains of a single substructure, fairly old and almost intact; this platform we identified as 32-G1 (Figure 17). To expose this platform we had to remove half of the height of Mound 32 and eliminate almost half of its horizontal extent.

The discovery of Structure 32-G1 was successful due to the many efforts by the workers and supervisors; they exercised great

Figura 16. Entierro 297 y cerámica de ofrenda. Arriba: solamente se aprecian los restos del cráneo deshecho 1: plato con borde ancho evertido y acanalado; cerámica con engobe rojo pulido; 2-4, 8-10: platos con engobe café-negruzco pulido; 5-7: plato y ollitas de cerámica cremosa pulida con manchas o bordes rojizos; 11: plato importado tipo Usulután ahumado negruzco.

Figure 16. Burial 297 and ceramic offerings. Above: just a few damaged cranial bones are apparent; 1. Flat-bottomed bowl with wide-everted, grooved rim and polished red slip; 2-4, 8-10. Bowls with polished black-brown slip; 5-7. Deep flat-bottomed bowl and small jars with polished cream slip and red rims; 11. Imported Usulután smoky black, flat-bottomed bowl.

se ejerció un gran cuidado al explorar los restos de muros y pisos donde gran parte de éstos se encontraron incompletos o faltantes. Básicamente, fue cuestión de establecer la forma original de varias escaleras y muchas esquinas, tanto interiores como exteriores, con lo cual se pudo identificar una gran estructura con planta arquitectónica en forma de "T", y con múltiples accesos a su superficie. Una vez encontrados los arranques de edificio, se procedió a la consolidación y restauración de la mampostería de la Plataforma G1. Al principio de la obra, los albañiles locales, quienes no conocían la técnica de reconstrucción arqueológica, trabajaron en conjunto con los encargados, pero rápidamente comprendieron la forma de colocar de nuevo las mismas piedras talladas recogidas en las excavaciones. La antigua mampostería de Chiapa de Corzo utilizaba únicamente una argamasa o mezcla de lodo, pero en la reconstrucción se aplicó una mezcla de cemento y cal, colocando un poco de lodo encima de las juntaras para evitar el fuerte contraste entre los materiales nuevos y viejos. También se taparon todas las grietas viejas con la nueva mezcla de cemento para su mejor conservación. En los taludes restaurados se colocó piedrín en las juntas de mezcla entre los bloques de piedra, lo cual dejó una marca claramente identificable a simple vista (Figuras 17 y 26).

Es conveniente describir el descubrimiento y restauración de la Estructura 32-G1 en orden, comenzando con sus diversas escalinatas y concluyendo con el patio y el edificio superior.

La Escalinata y la Esquina Noroeste

La esquina noroeste fue el primer elemento explorada durante las investigaciones. Hemos mencionado antes (Figura 12) la forma en que la ampliación de la carretera destruyó el muro occidental y la esquina noroeste de la Estructura G2, las cuales habían sido descubiertas casi completas en toda su altura y longitud. Antes de hacer esta limpieza del muro occidental se había excavado una entrada al lado norte del montículo (Figura 18) y se descubrieron solamente restos de los muros tardíos G4 y G3, pero el G1 (unido aquí con el G2) apareció intacto. Fue posible, entonces, seguir limpiando

care in exploring the remains of the walls and floors where a majority of these were incomplete or missing. It was basically a question of establishing the nature of the original form from the various stairways and corners, interior as well as exterior, with what could be identified as a large structure with a T-shaped architectural layout and multiple accesses to its surface. Once the initial remains of the structure were uncovered, consolidation and restoration of the masonry of Platform G1 began. At the beginning of this work, the local workmen, who were not familiar with techniques of archaeological restoration, worked together with the technicians and rapidly learned how to replace the worked stones recovered from the excavations. The ancient masonry of Chiapa de Corzo only utilized a mortar or mud mixture, but in the reconstruction work a mixture of cement and lime was applied. We placed just a bit of mud over the junctures to avoid a strong contrast between the ancient and restored sections of walls. Also, workers covered over all of the old cracks with the new mixture for better preservation. On the restored sloping walls or taluds they placed small stones in the joins between the blocks of stones, which left identifiable and visible marks (Figures 17, 26).

Here, we describe the discovery and restoration of Structure 32-G1 in order, beginning with its various stairways and concluding with the patio and upper building.

The Stairway and Northwest Corner

The northwest corner was the first element explored during the investigations. We have mentioned before (Figure 12) the way in which the expansion of the highway destroyed the west wall and the northwest corner of Structure G2, which had been uncovered almost intact in its height and length. Prior to the cleaning of the west wall, a point of access had been excavated on the north side of the mound (Figure 18). Although only sections of later walls G4 and G3 were discovered, G1 (combined here with G2) appeared intact. It was possible therefore to continue cleaning the backside of G1 (together

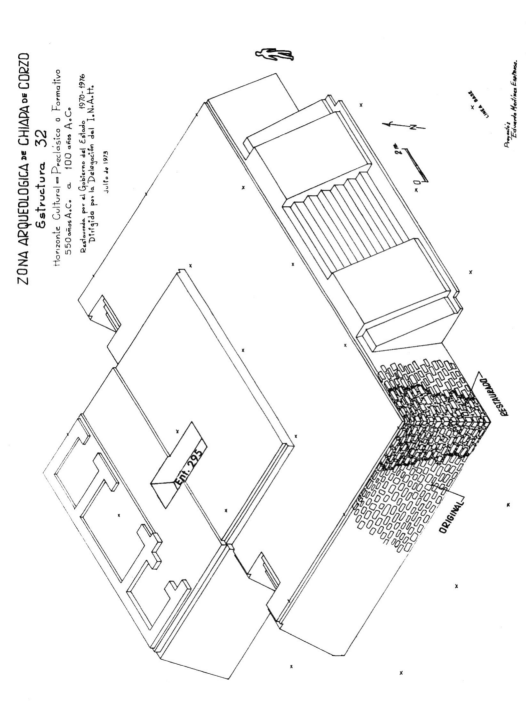

Figura 17. Reconstrucción isométrica de la Estructura 32 G-1. Este dibujo original fue proyectado por E. Martínez en 1973; se muestra el uso de piedritas en la mampostería restaurada en la consolidación de la Plataforma G-1. La tumba de Entierro 87 es intrusiva durante una etapa constructiva posterior.

Figure 17. Isometric reconstruction of Structure 32 G-1. This original drawing was done by Eduardo Martínez in 1973; it shows the use of small stones in the restored masonry of the consolidated Platform G-1. The tomb of Burial 87 was intruded into it during a subsequent construction stage.

Figura 18. Descubrimiento del lado norte del Montículo 32. Aparición del muro norte de la Plataforma 32 G-3 (atrás) y restos de muros G-4 (centro); Abajo: vista general del lado y la esquina noroeste después de su limpieza; hay que notar la incursión de la carretera a la derecha, lo que requirió la demolición de los muros G-2 y G-3.

Figure 18. The uncovering of the north side of Mound 32. Appearance of the north wall of Platform 32 G-3 (behind) and remains of wall G-4 (center). One can see the incursion of the highway in the inset, lower right hand corner, which required the demolition of walls G-2 and G-3.

Figura 19. Esquina noroeste de la Estructura 32 G-2. Mampostería de la esquina tal como se fue encontrando a quitar el relleno superpuesto de la Plataforma G-2; Abajo: el lado oeste antes de su demolición por el ensanchamiento de la nueva carretera.

Figure 19. Northwest corner of Structure 32 G-2. Masonry in the corner as it appeared when the overlying fill of Platform G-2 was removed; Below: the west side prior to its demolition for the widening of the new highway.

Figura 20. Descubrimiento y consolidación de la esquina noroeste de la Estructura 32 G-1; Descubrimiento de la escalera noroeste al retirar el relleno de la Plataforma G-2.

Figure 20. The exposure and consolidation of the northwest corner of Structure 32 G-1; Discovery of the northwest stairway upon the removal of fill from Platform G-2.

el muro trasero de G1 (junto con G2) hasta la esquina noroeste de G2 (Figuras 18, abajo, y 19; comparar el plano de la Figura 4).

En el momento de su excavación, la esquina noroeste y el muro occidental de la Estructura G2 eran una auténtica belleza, un ejemplo casi único de la arquitectura pública del periodo Preclásico Tardío, en excelente estado de conservación. A pesar de esta novedosa e importante categoría de la Plataforma G2, fue necesaria su casi inmediata demolición, como ya hemos explicado. A pesar de ello fue muy satisfactorio, en esta situación, ver aparecer una construcción aún más antigua dentro de la Plataforma G2, identificada como G1. La conservación de la Plataforma G1 no era tan perfecta como fue la de la G2, aunque todavía se mantenían algunos sectores intactos de talud a su máxima altura (Figura 20).

with G2) to the northwest corner of G2 (Figure 18, lower; Figure 19; compare with the map in Figure 4).

At the time of its excavation, the northwest corner and the west wall of Structure G2 were a genuine beauty, an almost unique example of public architecture from the Late Preclassic period in an excellent state of preservation. In spite of the exceptional state of preservation and importance of Platform G2, it was necessary to remove it immediately, as we have explained. In spite of the situation, it was satisfying to see the appearance of an even older construction within Platform G2, identified as G1. The preservation of Platform G1 was not as perfect as that of G2, although sectors of the talud were still intact to its maximum height (Figure 20).

Figura 21. Restauración terminada de la escalinata y la esquina noroeste.

Figure 21. Restoration completed of stairway and northwest corner.

Al retirar los muros y el relleno de la Plataforma G2 en su sector noroeste se apreció una reducción significativa en el ancho de la Plataforma G1, con una escalinata trasera remetida en el muro medial; todo ello sugería una duplicación de la planta arquitectónica en forma de "T", conocida en las plataformas del Montículo 1, en la sección sur del sitio (ver Figura 35). Sin embargo, los taludes simples de las Plataformas 32-G1 y 32-G2 parecían indicar un fechamiento anterior al del Montículo 1, que presentaba perfiles compuestos y que ha sido fechado para el periodo Protoclásico Temprano (fase Horcones o Chiapa VI). Esta conjetura fue confirmada con el descubrimiento de los dos entierros intrusivos hallados encima de la Plataforma G1, cuya ofrendas de cerámica fueron fechadas para el periodo Preclásico Tardío (fase Guanacaste o Chiapa V). Así, la Plataforma 32-G1 parece ser la antecesora inmediata de la Plataforma 1-H9 (Figura 35) dado que había sido construida unas décadas o, tal vez, hasta un siglo antes.

Al finalizar los trabajos fue posible restaurar completamente las esquinas y la

Upon removing the walls and fill of Platform G2 in the northwest section, a significant reduction in the width of Platform G1 was noted, with a rear stairway tapering off into the middle wall, all of which suggested a replication of the "T-shaped" architectural layout, similar to platforms in Mound 1 in the southern zone of the site (Figure 35). Nonetheless, the simple taluds or sloping exterior walls of Platforms 32-G1 and 32-G2 seemed to indicate an earlier date than those of Mound 1, which had composite profiles that had been dated to the early Protoclassic (Horcones or Chiapa VI phase). This conjecture was confirmed with the discovery of two intrusive burials on top of Platform G, with ceramic offerings dating to the Late Preclassic period (Guanacaste or Chiapa V phase). In addition, Platform 32-G1 seems to have been the immediate antecedent to Platform 1-H9 (Figure 35), given that it had been constructed some decades or perhaps up to a century before.

At the end of the excavation it was possible to completely restore the corners and the

Figura 22. Descubrimiento de la esquina y la escalinata noreste de la Estructura 32 G-1. Limpieza preliminar, con restos del muro noreste de la Estructura G-3 todavía visible al lado izquierdo.

Figure 22. Exposure of the corner and northeast stairway of Structure 32 G-1. Preliminary cleaning with the remains of the northeast wall of Structure G-3 still visible to the left side.

escalinata noroeste de la Estructura 32-G1 a su condición original, aunque sin recubrirlas de estuco (Figura 21).

Las Esquinas y la Escalinata Noreste con su Gran Basurero Ritual

Los primeros pasos de los tractores por el extremo noreste del Montículo 32 también revelaron restos de mampostería in situ (ver Figura 2b). El desescombro de los muros encontrados allí dejó rápidamente a la vista la situación que se presenta en la Figura 22; la Plataforma G1 también había sido enterrada en sus lados norte y este por las ampliaciones G2 y G3. La arquitectura del lado oriente mantuvo el mismo patrón arquitectónico de la planta en forma de "T", con otra escalinata trasera.

Aunque muy sumida y erosionada o saqueada antiguamente (Figura 23), la condición de la esquina noreste de la Plataforma G1

northwest stairway of Structure 32-G1 to its original condition, albeit without re-covering everything in stucco (Figure 21).

The Corners and the Northeast Stairway with its Large Ritual Deposit

The first passes by the tractors along the extreme northeast side of Mound 32 revealed traces of masonry in situ (see Figure 2b). The clean-up of the walls found there rapidly revealed the walls shown in Figure 22; Platform G1 had been buried on its north and east side with the extensions of Platforms G2 and G3. The architecture on the east side maintained the same architectural T-shaped layout, with another stairway behind it.

While deeply buried and eroded or looted in ancient times (Figure 23), the condition of the northeast corner of Platform G1 still allowed

Figura 23. Limpieza de la esquina noreste de G-1 terminada y esperando su restauración; al frente, abajo, se ve parte del gran basurero ritual.

Figure 23. Cleaning of the northeast corner of G-1 completed and awaiting restoration; in the front below, part of the of the great ritual trash deposit is visible.

todavía permitió una restauración a su estado original. Fue posible averiguar las medidas precisas de las gradas y restaurar fielmente la escalinata de acceso posterior. Los taludes y esquinas fueron restaurados siguiendo el ejemplo del mejor conservado lado noroeste, descrito arriba. Los resultados obtenidos aportaron así una plataforma casi perfectamente simétrica, como se puede apreciar en la Figura 28.

Al pie de la escalinata noreste, y corriendo al norte, parejo con el desplante del talud noreste de la extensión norte de la Estructura 32-G1, apareció un basurero ritual de gran extensión (Figuras 24 y 25). El basurero tenía el aspecto de una ofrenda por su tamaño y por la cantidad de material, obviamente depositado al momento de reconstruir o ampliar la estructura; sin embargo, ningún objeto entero o reconstruible fue recuperado (con la excepción de algunas manos de molienda). Este basurero incluyó:

restoration to its original state. It was possible to figure out the precise measurements of the steps and faithfully restore the rear access stairway. The slopes and corners were restored following the example of the better preserved northwest corner, as described above. The results supported the assessment of an almost perfectly symmetrical platform, as can be appreciated in Figure 28.

A ritual trash deposit was discovered at the foot of the northeast stairway and ran north, level with the foundation of the northeast slope from the north extension of Structure 32-G1 (Figures 24-25). The deposit seemed to be an offering, given its size and the quantity of material obviously deposited at the moment the structure was extended; however, no whole or reconstructible objects were recovered (with the exception of some manos). This deposit included:

Figura 24. Vista del gran basurero ritual de G-3. El basurero ritual en la base de la escalinata noreste de la Estructura G-1, en donde fue depositado antes de taparse con el relleno de la Plataforma G-3.

Figure 24. View of the great ritual trash deposit of G-3. The ritual trash deposit at the base of the northeast stairway of Structure G-3, which was deposited prior to covering Platform G-3 with fill.

Figura 25. Vista del basurero mirando al norte; ningún objeto
completo fue indentificado.

Figure 25. View of the trash deposit looking north; no complete object
was identified.

Figura 26. Limpieza y restauración del frente de la Estructura 32 G-1. Restaurando las dos alfardas con la escalinata principal todavía sin arreglar.

Figure 26. Cleaning and restoration of the front of Structure 32 G-1. Restoration of the two balustrades, with the principal stairway yet to have been done.

- 10 fragmentos de piedras de moler (manos, pedazos de metates y un disco grueso);

- Varios tiestos grandes de ollas y urnas enormes y pesadas;

- Muchos tiestos pequeños de recipientes.

La mejor interpretación que podemos ofrecer sobre este basurero es que se trata de los restos representativos de una gran fiesta o ceremonia dedicatoria, sin duda relacionada directamente con una ampliación de la arquitectura. Aunque fuese un evento que incluyera alimentos o bebidas embriagantes, ambos tendrían como ingrediente principal el maíz molido; por tratarse de una ceremonia sagrada, los implementos y los fragmentos de las ollas y vasijas fueron depositados al momento de enterrar la Plataforma 32-G1 en el relleno de la siguiente ampliación del edificio. Sin duda, hubo una destrucción ritual de todos los objetos utilizados antes de ser enterrados.

-10 fragments of grinding stones (manos, pieces of metates, and a thick, disc-shaped stone);

-Many sherds from jars and large, heavy urns;

-Many small sherds from bowls.

The best interpretation we can offer on this termination offering is that it is representative remains of a great feast or dedicatory ceremony, undoubtedly related directly to the architectural extension. Although it may have been an event that included foodstuffs or alcohol, both of these elements would have had ground maize as the principal ingredient. In terms of a sacred ceremony, the implements and vessel fragments were deposited at the moment of the interment of Platform 32-G1 under the fill of the subsequent building extension. No doubt, there would have been a ritual destruction of all the objects used prior to their burial.

Figura 27. Terminando la restauración de la esquina suroeste.

Figure 27. Finishing up the restoration in the southwest corner.

El Frente y la Escalinata Principal

Las excavaciones practicadas en el lado sur del Montículo 32 descubrieron una escalinata ancha con alfardas amplias que daban acceso al frente de la Estructura 32-G1 (Figura 26). Mucha piedra labrada había sido ya retirada de las gradas, las alfardas y los taludes antes de enterrar la estructura debajo el relleno de plataformas posteriores, pero afortunadamente quedaron restos suficientes para facilitar su restauración (ver Frontispicio y Figura 17). Las esquinas de la plataforma fueron elevadas a su altura original (Figura 23). La escalinata y las alfardas descansaban sobre una banqueta apenas perceptible, pero los bordes remetidos exteriores de las alfardas estaban claramente indicados; aquí, como en muchos otros elementos, los albañiles pudieron guiarse siguiendo el patrón de la muy parecida Estructura 1-H9 en el sur del sitio (Figura 35).

Según las observaciones de Martínez, se utilizó tanto el estuco de cal como el barro

The Front of the Mound and its Principal Stairway

Excavations undertaken on the south side of Mound 32 discovered a wide stairway with wide balustrades, which offered access to the front of Structure 32-G1 (Figure 26). Much worked stone had already been removed from the steps, the balustrades, and the exterior walls before the platform was buried under the construction fill of later platforms, but fortunately there was enough remaining to facilitate restoration (see Frontispiece and Figure 17). The corners of the platform were elevated to their original height (Figure 23). The stairway and balustrades rested on an almost imperceptible bench, but the exterior lower edges of the balustrades are clearly indicated. Here, as in many elements, the workmen were able to follow the pattern of the very similar Structure 1-H9 in the southern part of the site (Figure 35).

According to Martínez's observations, lime stucco as well as burned clay were used for the

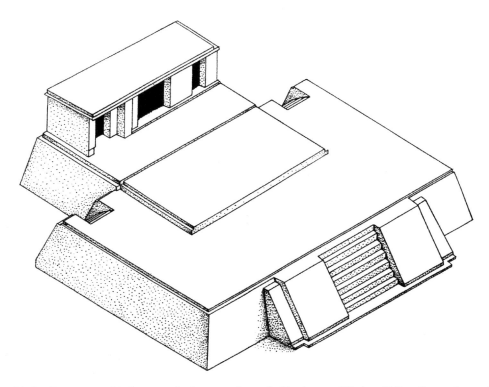

Figura 28. La Estructura 32 G-1, con la forma más probable de su edificio público ilustrada encima. Proyección isométrica del dibujante José Nuñez Chanona, basada en los datos de E. Martínez.

Figure 28. Structure 32 G-1, with the most likely public building type illustrated at the top. Isometric drawing by José Nuñez Chanona, based on the observations of Eduardo Martínez.

quemado para el revestimiento de las estructuras más antiguas de Chiapa de Corzo. Por lo regular, el repello de estas épocas era bastante delgado, aplicado sobre mampostería unida con mezcla de lodo, lo que por consecuencia facilitó la descomposición y rápida caída del recubrimiento al quedar enterrado debajo de la tierra y las piedras de un relleno sobrepuesto en las ampliaciones sucesivas tan comunes en la zona. Es raro encontrar evidencias del repello intacto en las ruinas, pero sí existen en partes bien protegidos, y no hay duda de que todos los edificios y subestructuras estaban así recubiertos originalmente.

facing on the oldest structures at Chiapa de Corzo. Typically, the plaster of these times was thin and applied on the masonry together with a mud mixture. This thin plaster, consequently, led to deterioration and collapse of the facing, which was then buried under the earth and stone fill of successive platform expansions so common to this site. It is rare to encounter evidence of intact facing on the ancient platforms, but it does exist in well-protected spots, and there is no doubt that all of the buildings and substructures were originally covered with fine plaster.

El Patio y los Edificios Superiores

Sobre la superficie de la Estructura 32-G1 se encontraron restos de un piso o pisos de estuco (todavía visibles en algunas partes del

The Patio and Upper Buildings

The remains of a stucco floor or floors were found in Structure 32-G1 (still visible in some sections of the building). In the central and

edificio). En la parte central y posterior de este piso se levantaron plataformas secundarias de 30 cm de altura (Figura 28). Sobre la plataforma trasera se apreciaban todavía los cimientos de un recinto de tres cuartos (ver Figura 7, restos a la izquierda). En algunas partes, los restos de los muros del edificio permanecían intactos hasta una altura de 50 cm. Con las evidencias que se han conservado es posible proyectar una reconstrucción artística de su probable aspecto original (Figura 28), con la ayuda de los datos mejor conservados procedentes de los edificios de la parte sur del sitio (Figura 36). La sencillez del pequeño edificio de tres cuartos nos permite suponer que fue utilizado como un templo para rituales sagrados; el amplio espacio abierto sobre la plataforma, enfrente del edificio, podría habido servido para los rituales públicos (ver la sección de Discusión).

ARTEFACTOS DEL RELLENO

Mientras avanzaba la exploración de las plataformas enterradas en el Montículo 32, todos los artefactos o tiestos de interés fueron registrados y conservados para su estudio y posterior entrega al Museo Regional (por general, los tiestos del relleno no se conservaron). En esta sección se reportan los materiales arqueológicos de mayor importancia.

Vasijas de Cerámica

En la Figura 29 aparece un conjunto de tres platos y parte de una olla, todos ellos corresponden a un tipo de cerámica bien acabada y pulida, probablemente de importación desde las regiones ocupadas por los mayas preclásicos en el noreste de Chiapas o Guatemala; no se conserva la procedencia exacta de estas vasijas, que seguramente componían una ofrenda de importancia, tal vez de categoría dedicatoria. Su estilo pertenece a los inicios de la fase Chicanel del periodo Preclásico Tardío. Se encontraron también varios tiestos de la misma época y origen mayance, aunque pintados en el estilo "bícromo" de líneas ondulantes o semi-circulares, generalmente de color rojo sobre crema (Figura 30). Otros tiestos y alguna vasija del mismo estilo han aparecido en diversas partes del sitio arqueológico de Chiapa de Corzo (por ejemplo,

back parts of this floor, secondary platforms of 30 cm in height were raised (Figure 28). At the back of the platform, the base or foundation of the three-room enclosure can still be seen (see Figure 7, remains to the left). In some sections, the remains of the walls of the structure remain intact up to a height of 50 cm. With the evidence available, an artistic reconstruction of its likely original state is possible (Figure 28), particularly with the help of better preserved data for structures in the southern zone of the site (Figure 36). The simplicity of the small three-room building suggests that it was used as temple for sacred rituals; the wide, open space on the platform in front of the structure could have served as a locale for public rituals (see Discussion section).

ARTIFACTS FROM THE FILL

While the exploration of the buried platforms in Mound 32 was advancing, all of the artifacts or sherds of interest were documented and saved for study and subsequently given to the Regional Museum of Chiapas (in general, the sherds from fill were not kept). In this section we report on the most important archaeological materials.

Ceramic Vessels

Figure 29 shows a group of three flat-bottomed bowls and sections of a jar, all corresponding to a well-finished and polished ceramic type, probably imported from Preclassic Maya areas in northeastern Chiapas or Guatemala; the exact location is not known, but surely these vessels were part of an important offering, perhaps a dedicatory cache. Their style pertains to the beginnings of the Chicanel phase of the Late Preclassic period. Also found were various Maya sherds from the same time period painted in a "bichrome" style with undulating lines or semi-circles, typically red-on-cream in color (Figure 30). Other sherds and one vessel of the same style have appeared in other areas of the archaeological site of Chiapa de Corzo (e.g.,

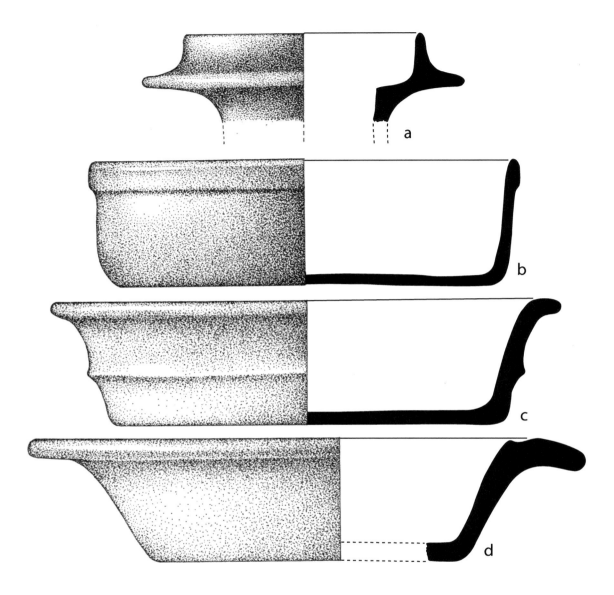

Figura 29. Vasijas de estilo Chicanel o maya preclásico recogidas del relleno del Montículo 32; a. boca de olla con engobe pulido color café-negruzco, b-d. vasijas con engobe rojizo pulido.

Figure 29. Chicanel style or Preclassic Maya vessels recovered from the fill of Mound 32; a. jar mouth with polished black-brown slip; b-d. vessels with polished red slip.

en el Montículo 15). Nos parece probable que tales tiestos representasen una clase de objetos de lujo utilizados por los antiguos pobladores como parte de su vida cotidiana, pero raramente incluidos en las ofrendas por no ser de la tradición zoqueana local (ver Discusión).

Sellos o Estampas de Cerámica

En el relleno se encontraron más de una docena de fragmentos de sellos o estampas de barro cocido (Figura 31, a-m). Los diseños de los sellos (Figura 32) muestran una semejanza lógica con muchos otros de Chiapa de Corzo, ya publicados por Lee (1969:71-86). Mayormente corresponden a la fase Francesa o Chiapa IV (finales del Preclásico Medio) y resultan así un poco anteriores a la construcción de la Estructura 32-G1. Supuestamente, los sellos sirvieron para decorar telas, madera o el cuerpo humano. Seguramente algunos fueron ideográficos, pero su posible significado ha sido poco estudiado; podrían presentar nombres de lugares y personas o representar conceptos cosmográficos.

Orejeras de Cerámica

Las cuatro orejeras de barro recuperadas (Figura 31, n-q), son cilíndricas y se parecen bastante a otras cuatro de Chiapa ya publicadas por Lee (1969: fig. 47, h-k), también de la fase Francesa, aparentemente. Las orejeras del Montículo 32 son sólidas y perforadas; una de ellas muestra una decoración incisa sencilla. Esta clase de orejeras duplica en cerámica la forma de las vértebras de pescado, comúnmente tiburón, utilizadas por varias culturas antiguas.

Anillos Dobles de Cerámica

En el rescate aparecieron fragmentos de cuatro o más "anillos dobles" de cerámica (Figura 31t, u). Son idénticos a unos 80 anillos, completos o fragmentados, reportados ya para Chiapa de Corzo (Lee 1969:71-73, figs. 34-35), mayormente de la fase Francesa. Aparentemente estos objetos sirvieron para atar la vestimenta; algunos de Chiapa de Corzo y de otros sitios tienen efigies de animales o personas en su anillo basal. Los anillos dobles se encuentran durante el Preclásico en muchas partes de Mesoamérica.

Mound 15). It seems likely to us that such sherds represent a class of luxury objects used by the ancient inhabitants as part of daily life but rarely included in offerings since they are not of local Zoque tradition.

Ceramic Seals or Stamps

More than a dozen fragments of fired clay seals or stamps were recovered from the mound fill (Figure 31 a-m). The seal designs (Figure 32) show an iconographic similarity with many others from Chiapa de Corzo, already published by Lee (1969:71-86). They mainly correspond to the Francesa or Chiapa IV phase (end of the Middle Preclassic period); therefore, they are older than the construction of Structure 32-G1. Seals may have been used to decorate cloth, wood, and the human body. Certainly some were ideographic, but their possible significance has been little studied. They could have depicted names of places or persons or represented cosmographic concepts.

Ceramic Earplugs

Four clay earplugs were recovered (Figure 31n-q); they are cylindrical and are similar to another four recovered at Chiapa de Corzo and published by Lee (1969: fig. 47h-k). They also apparently date to the Francesa phase. The earplugs are solid and perforated. One displays a simple incised design. This class of earplugs mimics the shape of fish vertebrae, commonly shark, used by many ancient cultures.

Ceramic Double Rings

During salvage work, fragments of four or more ceramic "double rings" were recovered (Figure 31t-u). They are identical to some 80 rings, whole and fragments, reported for Chiapa de Corzo (Lee 1969:71-73, figs. 34-35), chiefly from the Francesa phase. These objects were seemingly used to tie clothing. Some from Chiapa de Corzo and other sites are decorated with animal effigies or human characters. Double rings are found with Preclassic period remains in many parts of Mesoamerica.

0   2.5 cm

Figura 30. Tiestos bícromos de estilo Chicanel procedentes del relleno del Montículo 32. Mayormente están decorados con pintura roja-sobre-crema de probable importación de la zona maya de las tierras bajas y del periodo Preclásico Tardío.

Figure 30. Chicanel style bichrome sherds from the fill of Mound 32. They are primarily decorated with red-on-cream slip probably imported from the Maya Lowlands during the Late Preclassic period.

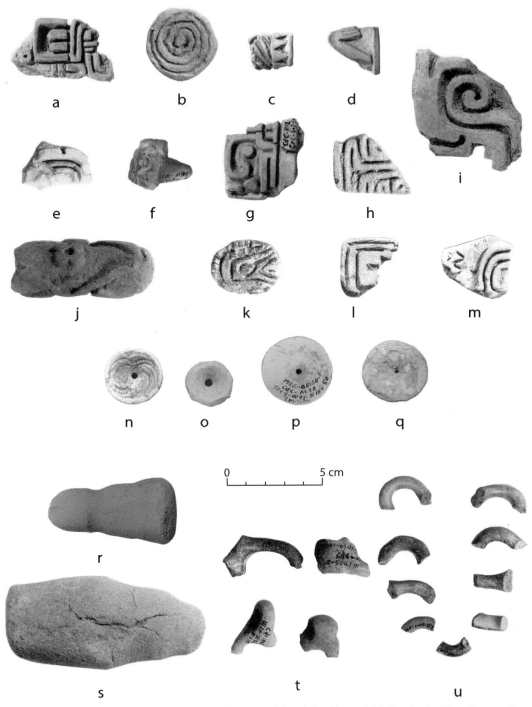

Figura 31. Sellos y otros artefactos de cerámica recogidos del relleno del Montículo 32. a, b, e-g, i, k-m: sellos planos con espiga; c, d, h, j: sellos cilíndricos (ver dibujos de los diseños en la Figura 32); n-q: orejeras de barro cocido, sólidas; n: con diseño esgrafiado; r-s: taladros de piedra; r. de piedra caliza, s. piedra arenisca con dos circunferencias de trabajo; t. fragmentos de "anillos dobles".

Figure 31. Seals and other ceramic artifacts recovered from the fill of Mound 32; a-b, e-g, i, k-m. Flat seals with a protruding stem; c-d, h, j: cylindrical seals (see design drawings in Figure 32); n-q: solid ceramic earplugs; n. with an incised design; r-s. carved from stone; r. limestone, s. sandstone with two circumferential grooves; t. fragments of "double rings."

Figura 32. Diseños de los sellos de cerámica.

Figure 32. Designs on the ceramic stamps.

0   5 cm

Figura 33. Figurillas de cerámica recogidas del relleno del Montículo 32. a: estilo olmeca temprano; b-e: estilo olmeca medio o "La Venta"; f-i: estilo olmeca tardío o fase Francesa de Chiapa de Corzo; j-l: estilos protoclásicos; m: figurilla zoomorfa, probablemente un perro.

Figure 33. Ceramic figurines recovered from the fill of Mound 32; a. Early Olmec style; b-e. Middle Olmec or "La Venta" style; f-i. Late Olmec style or Francesa phase from Chiapa de Corzo; j-l. Protoclassic styles; m. zoomorphic figure, probably a dog.

Taladros de Piedra

Dos taladros o barrenos de piedra, uno de arenisca y el otro de caliza, fueron recuperados en las excavaciones (Figura 31r, s). Son de buen tamaño por esta clase de herramienta (para tallar orificios de 2.5, 3.5 y 5 cm); tal vez sirvieran para fabricar orejeras tubulares. Doce barrenos de forma parecida y de distintos tamaños han sido recogidos en otras excavaciones en Chiapa de Corzo (Lee 1969: fig. 84), implicando la presencia de una industria lítica en la zona desde el Preclásico Temprano.

Figurillas de Cerámica

Más de 13 cabecitas de figurillas de barro cocido se recogieron en el relleno del Montículo 32 (Figura 33), además de un sinnúmero de fragmentos de cuerpos, brazos y piernas. Corresponden a todas las fases preclásicas, como se indica en la leyenda de la Figura 33, y presentan semejanzas con las más de 300 cabezas de figurillas de Chiapa de Corzo publicadas por Lee (1969:7-65). Todas las que proceden del Montículo 32 corresponden a estilos olmecas o zoqueanos preclásicos.

RESUMEN Y DISCUSIÓN

Seis semanas de salvamento arqueológico urgente a finales del año 1972, y otras semanas dedicadas a la restauración en 1973, pudieron lograr el rescate de una secuencia arquitectónica preclásica bastante compleja. También se logró la conservación y restauración de un monumento arqueológico más, que promueva el conocimiento prehispánico entre los chiapacorceños y los visitantes. La Estructura 32-G1 representa uno de las edificaciones más antiguas de todo México y es de las pocas tan fácilmente accesibles al público.

Los antiguos pobladores zoques del periodo Preclásico construyeron la Estructura 32-G1, y todas sus ampliaciones, antes de construir las estructuras del periodo Protoclásico encontradas en los Montículos 1 y 5, ahora consolidadas en la gran plaza, al sur del sitio. En Chiapa de Corzo se puede ver, así, el desarrollo arquitectónico de varios siglos de un pueblo muy activo y productivo en los siglos anteriores a nuestra era.

Stone Drills or Punches

Two stone drills or punches, one of sandstone and the other limestone, were recovered in the excavations (Figure 31r-s). They are of good size for this class of tools (to drill openings of 2.5, 3.5, and 5 cm for beads or other items). Perhaps they were used to create tubular ear flares. Twelve drills of similar form and different sizes have been collected from other excavations at Chiapa de Corzo (Lee 1969: fig. 84), implying the presence of a lithic industry in the zone since the Early Preclassic period.

Ceramic Figurines

More than 13 clay figurine heads were recovered in the fill of Mound 32 (Figure 33), in addition to numerous body, arm, and leg fragments. They date to all Preclassic periods, as noted in the caption of Figure 33, and are similar to the more than 300 figurine heads from Chiapa de Corzo published by Lee (1969:7-65). Those from Mound 32 correspond to Olmec and Preclassic Zoque styles.

SUMMARY AND DISCUSSION

After six weeks of emergency archaeological salvage work at the end of 1972, and an additional few weeks of restoration in 1973, we were able to save a fairly complex Preclassic architectural sequence. We also successfully preserved and restored one more archaeological monument to further Prehispanic knowledge for visitors and the people of Chiapa de Corzo. Structure 32-G1 represents one of the most ancient structures in all of Mexico and is one of the most easily accessible to the public.

The ancient Zoque inhabitants of the Preclassic period built Structure 32-G1, and all of its extensions, prior to the structures of the Protoclassic period found in Mounds 1 and 5, now consolidated in the great plaza in the southern area of the site. At Chiapa de Corzo one can also see the architectural development over the centuries of a very active and productive people before our Common Era.

A nuestro saber, la Estructura 32-G1 es el primer ejemplo de una plataforma alta construida con una planta arquitectónica en forma de "T". Este tipo de basamento para templos tuvo una extensa popularidad; las plataformas basales en forma de "T" presentaban al público un frente ancho e impresionante, mientras restringían la parte posterior, que soportaba el templo. Esta práctica limitaba el acceso al lugar más sagrado o más elitista del recinto.

La Plataforma 32-G1, en su sección delantera, mide aproximadamente 22 m de ancho en su base, con 15 m de profundidad en cada lado, mientras que la extensión posterior, más reducida, solamente tiene 12 m de ancho por 6 m de profundidad. La superficie de la plataforma está ligeramente reducida por la pendiente de los taludes y por una grada superior, con lo cual su extensión total de piso es de aproximadamente 285 m², de los cuales 58 m² corresponden a la extensión trasera. El templo medía 4 m de ancho por 10.5 de largo y ocupaba apenas 42 m². La escalera delantera presenta siete gradas, con una anchura total de 4.5 m, y ambas alfardas miden también 4.5 m de grosor, pero con un metro exterior de cada alfarda remetido formando una franja hundida; todo está asentado sobre una banqueta baja que se extiende al sur de la plataforma, a unos 2.5 m en su base.

La Estructura 32-G4 ¿Un Monumento Funerario?

La gran plataforma 32-G4 que cubrió completamente a la G1, junto con todas sus primeras etapas constructivas, tiene que ser entendida en cierto momento como un monumento funerario de mucha categoría en la comunidad. No tenemos datos del exterior o la superficie de la Estructura 32-G4 (desaparecidos por la erosión natural y el saqueo de materiales), pero sí sabemos que los constructores originales mantuvieron abierto una gran oquedad en su centro (Figura 34) mientras se terminaba la edificación de los grandes taludes exteriores con miles de bloques de piedra tallada. Esta práctica indica, sin duda, el alto prestigio de la persona a quien iba a enterrar dentro de la plataforma del templo.

To our knowledge, Structure 32-G1 is the first example of a tall platform constructed with a "T-shaped" layout. This type of base for temples enjoyed wide popularity. The "T-shaped" platform bases presented a wide and impressive front to the public, while restricting the back section supporting the temple. This practice limited access to the more sacred and elite areas of the precinct.

Platform 32-G1, in its front section, measures approximately 22 m in width at its base, with a 15 m length on each side, while the rear section, much reduced, is only 12 m in width with only 6 m in depth. The platform surface is slightly reduced due to the degree of the slope and also by the uppermost step. There is a total floor surface of 285 m², of which 58 m² is the back extension. The temple on top measures 4 m in width by 10.5 m in length and occupies just 42 m². The front stairway has seven steps with a width of 4.5 m, and both balustrades also measure 4.5 m in width with a meter beyond each inset section. The entire front of the structure sits on a bench or low platform that extends south of the platform, some 2.5 m at its base.

Structure 32-G4: A Funerary Monument?

The large 32-G4 platform that completely covers G1, together with all of its first stages of construction, should be understood as a high-status funerary monument of the community at a particular moment. We have no data from the exterior or surface of Structure 32-G4 (which disappeared due to erosion and looting of materials), but we do know that the original builders maintained the great cavity in its center (Figure 34) while finishing the construction of the great exterior slopes with thousands of shaped stone blocks. This practice undoubtedly indicates the high prestige of the person who was to be interred within the temple platform.

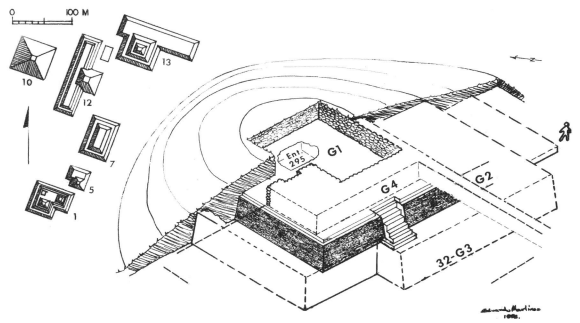

Figura 34. Costumbres funerarias en la arquitectura preclásica de Chiapa de Corzo. Izquierda: centro ceremonial principal del sitio de Chiapa de Corzo; la Estructura 1 contenía seis tumbas de los periodos Preclásico Tardío y Protoclásico. Derecha: secuencia idealizada de la arquitectura del Montículo 32, donde se muestra la función del "patio hundido" para recibir la tumba y el Entierro 87 al construir la etapa G-4, la última de la fase Guanacaste. Dibujo adaptado de un bosquejo de E. Martínez preparado en 1972 al inicio de las excavaciones.

Figure 34. Funerary customs in Preclassic architecture at Chiapa de Corzo. Left: principal ceremonial center of Chiapa de Corzo; Structure 1 contained six tombs from the Late Preclassic and Protoclassic periods. Right: Idealized sequence of Mound 32 showing the "sunken patio" for receiving the tomb and Burial 87 with the construction of Stage G-4, the last of the Guanacaste phase. Drawing adapted from a sketch by Eduardo Martínez prepared in 1972 at the beginning of the excavations.

Una vez que fue tapada la tumba del Entierro 87, podríamos suponer que entonces se rellenó el "patio hundido" y se procedió a la nivelación de un piso de estuco superior, que sostendría uno o más edificios. Es casi seguro, además, que los sacerdotes-nobles del lugar aprovecharían la memoria del personaje allí depositado con el fin de inculcar el respeto a sus rituales o a los derechos heredados del difunto. Mientras que fuera asunto de preocupación el problema de la legitimidad de la herencia o la fidelidad, se mantendría vivo el recuerdo del personaje fallecido; en esta época se puede pensar en la estructura que conservaba los restos como un monumento fúnebre. Antes y después

Once the tomb of Burial 87 was sealed, we imagine the "sunken patio" was then filled and the area leveled and capped with a later stucco floor that supported one or two buildings. It is almost certain that nobles-priests of this place would have taken advantage of the memory of the individual buried there to instill respect for rituals or the hereditary rites conferred on the deceased. While there was concern for the problem of the legitimacy of heirs, the memory of the deceased lord would be maintained. For this era one can understand the preserved structure as a funerary monument. Before and after this era, it is doubtful that the Mound 32 platform was appreciated specifically as a

de tal época es dudoso que la plataforma fuese apreciada especialmente por su papel funerario. Es decir, a nuestro modo de pensar, las plataformas preclásicas tuvieron como función principal la de sustentar edificios públicos con fines rituales, y solamente en forma secundaria sirvieron para recibir o conmemorar a los líderes fallecidos. Concluimos así, por la distribución errática de entierros en las plataformas exploradas hasta el momento, que no puede discernirse un patrón claro.

Nos enfrentamos entonces con la cuestión, ¿los antiguos arquitectos hicieron las ampliaciones a sus plataformas por razones accidentales —crecimiento de población, familia, poder, fallecimiento de personajes importantes— o por obedecer reglas ceremoniales o cíclicas? Es siempre posible que todo cambio de época o fin de ciclo religioso requiriese forzosamente del cambio o la ampliación a alguna estructura arquitectónica, pero estamos convencidos de que el proceso fue bastante casual y que obedecía a factores locales muy variables. Tal falta de formalidad, visible en las costumbres funerarias de los pobladores preclásicos, no significa que sus exequias no fuesen ocasiones de gran importancia ceremonial; es obvio que las inhumaciones en las tumbas de Chiapa se acompañaron con rituales dignos de los más altos funcionarios.

Tanto en el caso del Entierro 87, colocado debajo de la Plataforma 32-G4, como en la Tumba 6 del Montículo 1 (Figura 35), los antiguos zoques de Chiapa de Corzo dejaron amplio espacio para llevar a cabo cualquier rito funerario. Para el Entierro 87, los constructores originales hicieron un ancho acceso del lado norte o trasero del "patio hundido", el cual fue cubierto en la misma forma con altos muros de retención hechos de piedra bola (ver Figura 4). Esta entrada llegaba directamente al pie de la tumba (Figuras 8 y 9a). La única justificación para tan formal entrada y para los 70 m² de superficie dejados temporalmente abiertos en este recinto hundido (Figura 8), es que fue diseñado específicamente para dar acceso y acomodar una procesión funeraria a la cripta.

De igual manera, en la Estructura 1-H9 del Montículo 1 (Figura 35) se dejó un espacio amplio similar para los ritos

funerary monument. That is to say, in our way of thinking the principal function of Preclassic platforms was to support public buildings for ritual ends and only served secondarily as burial places or commemorations for fallen leaders. We conclude this based on the erratic distribution of burials in the platforms explored to date for which we cannot discern a clear pattern.

We are then confronted with the question: Did the ancient architects undertake extensions of the platforms for incidental reasons—population growth, family power, deaths of important individuals—or to obey ceremonial rules of ritual cycles? It is always possible that each change of religious era or time cycle would require a change or addition to some architectural structure, but we are convinced that the process was coincidental and complied with variable local factors. Such a lack of formality in the funerary customs of the Preclassic inhabitants does not mean that such funeral rites were not of great ceremonial importance. It is obvious that the interments in the Chiapa de Corzo tombs were accompanied by rituals worthy of the highest status individuals.

For the case of Burial 87, located under Platform 32-G4, as well as for Tomb 6 of Mound 1 (Figure 35), the ancient Zoques of Chiapa de Corzo left a spacious area to carry out funerary rites. For Burial 87, the original builders created a wide access on the north side, behind the "sunken patio," which was covered with high retaining walls of stone cobbles (see Figure 4). This entrance led directly to the foot of the tomb (Figures 8, 9a). The only justification for such a formal entrance and for some 70 m² of surface temporarily left open in this sunken patio (Figure 8) is that it was designed especially to provide access for a funerary procession to the crypt.

In the same way, a similarly wide space for funerary rites was left in Structure 1-H9 of Mound 1 (Figure 35). We imagine groups

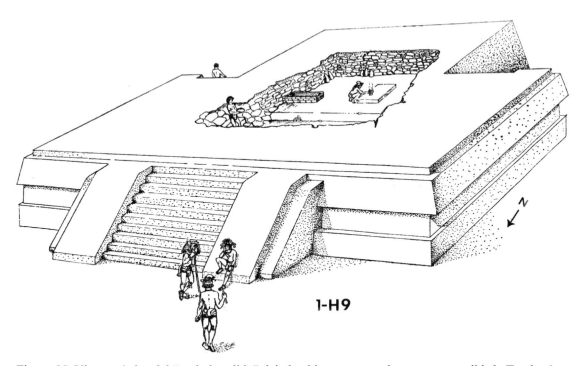

1-H9

Figura 35. Vista artística del "patio hundido" dejado abierto temporalmente para recibir la Tumba 6 en Estructura 1-H9, la primera construcción de la fase Horcones; se nota claramente el paralelismo con la Estructura 32 G-4. Dibujo de Pierre Agrinier (Lowe y Agrinier 1960: fig. 11).

Figure 35. Artistic reconstruction of the "sunken patio" temporarily left open to receive Tomb 6 in Structure 1-H9, the first construction of the Horcones phase; one can clearly see the parallels with Structure 32G-4. Drawing by Pierre Agrinier (Lowe and Agrinier 1960: fig. 11).

funerarios; podemos imaginar, además, grupos de participantes ubicados arriba, en las orillas del espacio que se dejó abierto. Los baseros en forma de plato, con tres picos al interior, figuraban en ambas ofrendas de los Entierros 87 y 88 en el Montículo 32, y esta clase de incensarios fue aún más común en los escondites dedicatorios protoclásicos encontrados en el Montículo 1 (Lowe y Agrinier 1960: figs. 56, 58, 60, 63; láms. 31-33, 36-37). La persistente quema de resinas aromáticas u otros elementos confirma el carácter sagrado de las ceremonias relacionadas con los entierros y las ampliaciones arquitectónicas.

of participants located around the edges of the open space. The three-horned plate-shaped censers were prominent in offerings for both Burials 87 and 88 in Mound 32, and this class of censer was even more common in Protoclassic dedicatory caches found in Mound 1 (Lowe and Agrinier 1960: figs. 56, 58, 60, 63, pls. 31-33, 36-37). The persistent burning of aromatic resins and other elements confirm the sacred character of the ceremonies related to the burials and architectural extensions.

El Edificio 32-G1 ¿Templo o Palacio?

Hemos identificado como un templo al pequeño edificio construido encima de la Estructura 32-G1, precisamente por el poco

Building 32-G1: Temple or Palace?

We have identified the small building constructed on top of Structure 32-G1 as a small temple precisely because of the small space

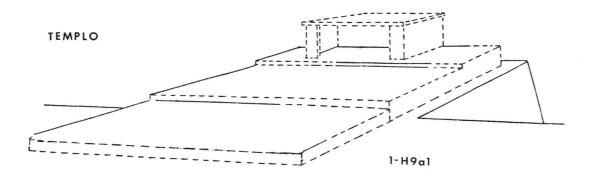

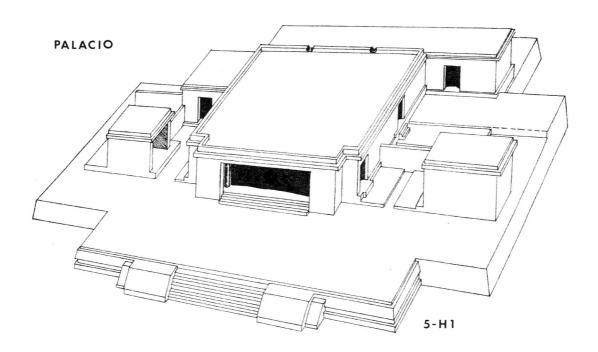

Figura 36. Arquitectura "religiosa" y "cívica" en Chiapa de Corzo durante el periodo Protoclásico Temprano. a. un "templo" de un solo cuarto, el primer edificio construido sobre la Plataforma 1-H9 (Lowe y Agrinier 1960: fig. 12). b. el "palacio" de once cuartos, construido sobre la Plataforma 5-H1 al final de la fase Horcones (Lowe 1962: frontispicio).

Figure 36. "Religious" and "civic" architecture at Chiapa de Corzo during the early Protoclassic period; a. "temple" with one room, the first building constructed on Platform 1-H9 (Lowe and Agrinier 1960: fig. 12); b. "palace" of eleven rooms, constructed on Platform 5-H1 at the end of the Horcones phase (Lowe 1962: frontispiece).

espacio encerrado en sus tres cuartos y por estar ubicado en un "lugar sagrado" de acceso limitado, que se extendía por detrás de la plataforma principal (ver Figura 28). Hay otro caso idéntico en la Estructura 1-H9a1 del Montículo 1, en la plaza sur del sitio (Figura 36a); la Plataforma 1-H9 es un poco más reciente que las Plataformas 32-G1 a G4, pero mantiene la misma tradición arquitectónica básicamente sin interrupción. Ambas series de plataformas están elevadas hasta 3 m por encima del nivel de sus plazas.

Por otra parte, un edificio superior de Chiapa de Corzo que sí logramos identificar como un palacio es la Estructura 5-H1 del Montículo 5 (Figura 36b). La estructura basal o plataforma primaria mantiene la planta arquitectónica en forma de "T" o de cruz con las esquinas remetidas, pero es relativamente baja; en cambio, la estructura o edificio superior resultaba sumamente compleja en su trazo, con once cuartos y varios patios pequeños. Había dos salas de recepción de tamaño regular y una serie de antecámaras y almacenes (ver detalles en Lowe 1962:7-18, fig. 2, láms. 1-5). La Estructura 5-H1 obviamente resulta muy diferente de la contigua Estructura 1-H9a1, y seguramente tenía una función más residencial (de élite, por supuesto). Considerando su proximidad y sus características tan diferentes, no resulta probable que ambas estructuras (1-H9 y 5-H1) fuesen templos (aunque evidentemente los edificios religiosos tanto como las residencias de los dignatarios podrían variar en forma y tamaño según sus funciones particulares o patrones específicos).

Las plataformas basales o primarias en sí podrían sostener cualquier clase de superestructura o edificio, mientras que las plataformas piramidales deben haber sostenido siempre edificios oficiales de los gobernantes. Desde el Preclásico Medio todo centro de población tenía una o dos pirámides y podemos pensar en ellas como asientos de linajes. Las plataformas basales, anchas y masivas, también son típicas del desarrollo formativo en el sureste de México. Las más antiguas plataformas grandes conocidas en Yucatán, por ejemplo, se

enclosed within its three rooms and its location within a "sacred space" with limited access, which extended behind the principal platform (see Figure 28). There is another identical case in Structure 1-H9a1 at Mound 1 in the south plaza of the site (Figure 36a). Platform 1-H9 is younger than Platforms 32-G1a to G4, but it generally maintained the same architectural tradition without interruption. Both series of platforms are elevated up to 3m above the level of their plazas.

What's more, a superstructure at Chiapa de Corzo that we were successful in identifying as a palace is Structure 5-H1 of Mound 5 (Figure 36b). The primary base structure or platform maintained the T-shape or cross architectural layout with inset corners, but it was relatively low. Nonetheless, the structure or upper building was extremely complex in its outline, with eleven rooms and various small patios. It had two regular-sized reception rooms and series of antechambers and storage rooms (see details in Lowe 1962:7-18, fig. 2, pls. 1-5). Structure 5-H1 was obviously very different from the nearby Structure 1-H9a1 and surely had a more residential function (elite, of course). Considering its proximity and its distinct characteristics, it is unlikely that both structures (1-H9 and 5-H1) were temples (although evidently religious buildings as well as residences of dignitaries could vary in form and size according to particular functions or specific patterns).

Basal or primary platforms, in essence, could have supported whatever class of superstructure or building, while pyramidal platforms would always have held official buildings of the rulers. Since the Middle Preclassic, every population center had one or two pyramids, and we think of them as seats of lineages. The base platforms, wide and massive, were also typical of Formative developments in southeastern Mexico. The largest and oldest platforms known in Yucatan, for example, come

acercan mucho a las de Chiapa de Corzo por sus taludes sencillos y la utilización de piedra cortada. Hay un desarrollo parecido en otras zonas mayas, aunque poco esclarecido aún por las investigaciones.

Ninguna región de Mesoamérica puede pretender ser dueña de los inicios de la arquitectura ceremonial: Chiapas tuvo plataformas de piedra cortada con recubrimiento de estuco desde cuando menos la fase Francesa (ca. 500 años a.C.), y algunas plataformas elevadas de barro y tierra compactada existieron desde la fase Barra, junto con la primera cerámica de Chiapas (ca. 1800 a.C.). Nos parece probable que la arquitectura se desarrolló de manera bastante pareja en muchas partes de Mesoamérica, una situación indicativa de una comunicación fácil y constante entre los pueblos. Los materiales, y a veces la decoración de las construcciones, variaron según el lugar, pero las normas arquitectónicas lo hicieron muy poco hasta el periodo Clásico.

Aportes Culturales de los Artefactos

Los escasos artefactos recuperados del relleno del Montículo 32 y la cerámica de las ofrendas asociadas a los entierros nos enfrenta a un hecho sobresaliente: los zoques preclásicos eran una población muy conservadora y tradicional. Media docena de vasijas completas y una docena de tiestos bícromos demuestran cierto contacto con sus vecinos más al norte y el oriente, pero los demás objetos son locales y poco variados (una ollita importada desde Mirador, 50 km al oeste, es también un producto zoqueano). Lo que se puede considerar como "humildad" o pobreza en los ajuares funerarios de las tumbas es clara indicación de que los difuntos eran personajes locales de una importancia tradicional; se rechazaba toda influencia de otra cultura. Además, era el contenido de las vasijas lo que importaba y no los objetos en sí mismos. Los fallecidos llevaban alimentos, bebidas y resinas aromáticas para su viaje al más allá. De la misma manera, podemos destacar la sencillez del gran basurero ritual depositado atrás de la Estructura 32-G1 antes de enterrarlo (Figuras 24 y 25); aquí también encontramos un énfasis total en comida y bebida.

close to those of Chiapa de Corzo with their simple slopes and use of cut stone. There was a similar development in other Maya zones, although still not well clarified by investigations to date.

No region of Mesoamerica can claim to be the owner of the beginnings of ceremonial architecture: Chiapas had platforms of cut stone covered in stucco starting at least by the Francesca phase (circa 500 BC), and some elevated platforms of clay and compacted earth existed in the Barra phase, together with the first ceramics of Chiapas (circa 1800 BC). It seems likely that architecture was developed in partnership throughout Mesoamerica, a situation indicative of easy and constant communication among peoples. The materials and sometimes the decoration of the constructions varied according to place, but the architectural norms changed little until the Classic period

Cultural Contributions from the Artifacts

The few artifacts recovered from the Mound 32 fill and ceramic offerings associated with the burials lead us to confront an obvious fact: the Preclassic Zoques were a very conservative and traditional population. A half dozen complete vessels and another dozen bichrome sherds demonstrate contact with their neighbors to the north and west, but the rest of the objects are local and show little variety (a small imported jar from Mirador, 50 km to the west, is still a Zoque product). What might be considered humble or poor in the funerary offerings of the tombs is clear indication that the deceased were local individuals of great importance; they rejected all influence from other cultures. In addition, it was the contents of the vessels that was important, not the vessels themselves. The deceased had foodstuffs, drinks, and aromatic resins for their trip to the great beyond. Similarly, we can highlight the simplicity of the great ritual deposit behind Structure 32-G1 prior to its interment (Figures 24-25); here also we find a total emphasis on food and drink.

Igualmente sencilla e informal fue la Tumba 6 de la fase Horcones enterrada en la gran oquedad dejada temporalmente en la Estructura 1-H9 del Montículo 1 (Figura 35), arriba mencionada; al fijarnos en la similitud de este entierro con el Enterrio 87 del Montículo 32, una ofrenda sencilla de tipo zoqueano es la que se esperaría. El individuo de la Tumba 6 llevaba un buen collar de jade con un colgante efigie de pico de pato, pero le acompañaban solamente ocho platitos, una olla y un tecomate sencillo (Lowe y Agrinier 1960:46-47, fig. 45, láms. 22-23). En la Tumba 6 se trata también de un personaje joven, netamente zoque de clara descendencia olmeca, como indica el colgante de jade en forma de cabeza de pato.

De fuerte contraste fue la Tumba 7 de la fase Guanacaste, enterrada un poco antes de construir la Plataforma 1-H con su Tumba 6. Aquí el rico ajuar funerario no contenía un solo objeto de claro origen local (aunque sí habían cinco platitos zoqueanos de la costa de Veracruz). La ofrenda incluía vasijas, obsidiana, pedernal, mica y jade, objetos todos importados desde Veracruz, Oaxaca, el Petén y los altos de Guatemala o El Salvador. Esta tumba, la más antigua del Montículo 1, obviamente correspondía a algún personaje rico o de mucha fama y no muy grande de edad; tal vez era un jefe-guerrero. Muy significativamente, la cercana Tumba 1, ya de la fase Horcones (y compañera al poco tiempo de la más simple Tumba 6, con su ofrenda estilo local), mantuvo la costumbre rival de incluir en su ofrenda gran cantidad de objetos de importación, entre ellos una lanza grande con una impresionante punta de obsidiana guatemalteca (Lowe y Agrinier 1960, figs. 36-37, láms. 18-19).

Así, las investigaciones en el antiguo asentamiento de Chiapa de Corzo hacen patente un alto nivel de desarrollo social para la sociedad zoqueana, ya en los siglos anteriores a nuestra era. Al parecer había una fuerte diferenciación de clases y ocupaciones, y tal vez artesanos de tiempo completo. La gran cantidad de piedra labrada en las estructura de Chiapa, por ejemplo, necesitaba muchos canteros tanto como albañiles, sobrestantes y arquitectos. Otros proyectos posteriores de salvamento en Chiapa de Corzo han demostrado una extensa gama de

Tomb 6 of the Horcones phase, placed in the large temporary cavity in Structure 1-H9 of Mound 1, was equally simple and informal (Figure 35), as previously mentioned. Noting the similarity of this burial with Burial 87 of Mound 32, a simple Zoque offering is what one would expect. The individual in Tomb 6 had a good jade necklace with an effigy duckbill pendant hanging from it, but he was accompanied by only eight small bowls, a jar, and a simple tecomate (Lowe and Agrinier 1960:46-47, fig. 45, pls. 22-23). The individual in Tomb 6 was a young person, clearly Zoque of Olmec descent, as indicated by the jade duckhead pendant.

Guanacaste phase Tomb 7 offers a strong contrast, buried just before the construction of Platform 1-H with Tomb 6. Here, the rich burial furniture did not contain a single object of clear local origin (although it did have five small Zoque bowls from the Veracruz coast). The offerings included vessels, obsidian, chert, mica, and jade, all objects imported from Veracruz, Oaxaca, the Petén, and the highlands of Guatemala or El Salvador. This tomb, the oldest in Mound 1, obviously pertains to an elite person of great fame and one who was not very old, perhaps a warrior-chief. Significantly, nearby Tomb 1, already from the Horocones phase (and coeval with the simpler Tomb 6), continued the competing custom of including among the offerings a great number of imported items, among them a spear with an impressive obsidian spearhead of Guatemalan obsidian (Lowe and Agrinier 1960: figs. 36-37, pls. 18-19).

And so, the investigations in the ancient settlement of Chiapa de Corzo have made clear the high level of social development in Zoque society already in place in the centuries before the Common Era. There seems to have been strong class and occupational distinctions, with perhaps full-time craftspersons. The great quantity of worked stone in the construction at the site, for example, would have required many quarry workers, as well as masons, overseers, and architects. Subsequent salvage projects at Chiapa de Corzo have demonstrated a wide

tipos de plataformas domésticas con variadas actividades artesanales.

Seguramente nos queda mucho por aprender sobre la antigua sociedad zoqueana, y no hay mejor lugar para lograrlo que en Chiapa de Corzo mismo. Una vigilancia constante para conservar o rescatar los datos aún disponibles en Chiapa de Corzo se encuentra claramente justificada. El desarrollo de más proyectos de investigación arqueológica en este sitio podrá ampliar profundamente nuestro entendimiento de una de las más antiguas y más interesantes ciudades en toda Mesoamérica.

range of domestic platform types offering a variety of artisan styles.

Surely there is much to learn about ancient Zoque society, and there is no better place for learning it than Chiapa de Corzo. Constant vigilance in preserving or rescuing the available data from the site is clearly justified. The development of more archaeological research projects here would greatly expand our understanding of one of the most ancient and interesting cities in all of Mesoamerica.

APPENDIX

ARTIFACTS FROM MOUND 32

John E. Clark, Artemio Villatoro Alvarado, and Juan Carlos López Espinosa

As apparent in the preceding report, Eduardo Martínez and Gareth Lowe did not study the artifacts from the Mound 32 salvage excavations in detail. Our purpose here is to provide information on most of these artifacts. We begin with objects from burials and then consider artifacts found in the general excavations. As to burial goods, it is important to note that not all were available for study and inclusion here. After completion of the Mound 32 salvage and restoration work, the main tomb was prepared for viewing by the public, and some artifacts were on display there for several years (Burial 295, now considered Burial 87 and Tomb 12). The tomb was eventually closed and the artifacts taken to the regional museum in Tuxtla Gutiérrez. We describe artifacts that were placed in the temporary care of the NWAF and are in the records of previous inventory.

We undertook the task of studying artifacts from Mound 32 after finishing a study of artifacts from Mound 15, located southeast of Mound 32. We follow much of the format of the Mound 15 monograph in our descriptions of those of Mound 32 (Glauner et al. 2017). The few comparisons we make are of the artifacts of these two mounds. Both were salvaged the same year, and both mounds were in the same quadrant of Chiapa de Corzo affected by the expansion of the Nestlé company. The mounds also both saw significant use and building activity in the Guanacaste phase, hence there are many similarities in their artifact inventories. Also remarkable are signal differences that may have to do with their specific functions. Mound 15 covered three low Guanacaste platforms used for residences (Glauner et al. 2017), and as described by Martínez and Lowe in their report, Mound 32 appears to have been a special temple at this time. Some of the artifacts found in the fills of this structure and the general excavations have not previously been reported for Chiapa de Corzo.

We do not attempt broad comparisons of artifacts here; our objectives are to describe, illustrate, and provide information for important or unusual objects. We begin with items from burials, which consist mostly of whole ceramic vessels, and then present artifacts from general excavations, beginning with ceramic artifacts and ending with stone artifacts. Most of the artifacts have individual numbers, and we list information according to these numbers. These are "MRE" numbers, meaning "Museo Regional del Estado," the regional museum of the Instituto Nacional de Antropología e Historia (INAH). All the information on file with the NWAF is according to this reference system. For the sake of clarity, for the few artifacts lacking numbers we insert "(sn)" in place of a number, meaning *sin número.*

ARTIFACTS FROM BURIALS AND CACHES
Burial 87 (Figures A1-A3)

Martínez and Lowe list six ceramic vessels, a marine shell, and two beads as the mortuary goods found with Burial 295, published with a new number (Burial 87, aka Tomb 12) in the Chiapa de Corzo system here because "295" and "296" had already been used for last-minute burials removed months earlier in Mound 15 (Glauner et al. 2017). Of the six vessels from Burial 87, we have pieces of four vessels and also a whole vessel not reported. The unreported bowl is one of the most interesting vessels found in the Mound 32 excavations. Its excavation tag describes it as "Vessel 4 from Burial 295," and this information was recorded in November of 1972; thus, this information was recorded at the time of the excavation. Martínez and Lowe list a small, footed jar with a spout as Vessel 4. There was clearly a labeling problem with these two candidates for Vessel 4 and difficulty in keeping track of all items that came from

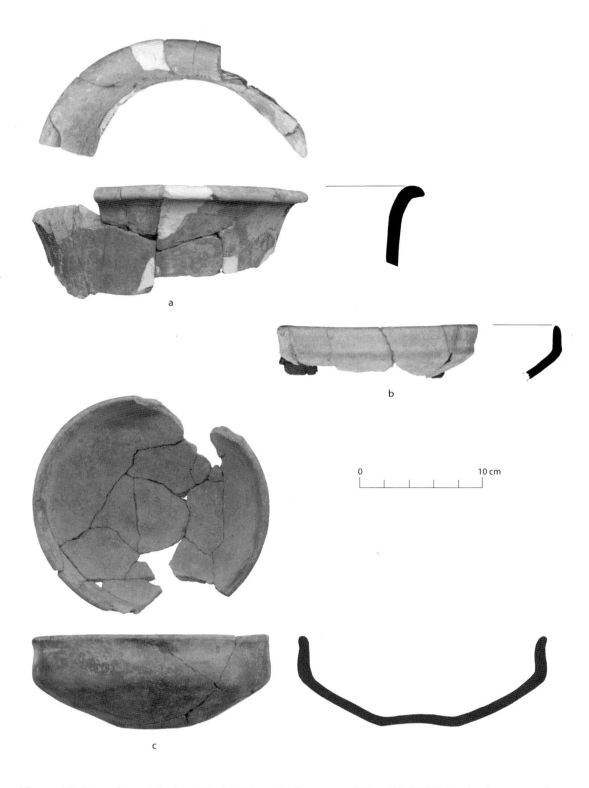

Figure A1. Ceramic vessels from Burial 87; a. rim fragment of Vessel 1 (5304), b. rim fragment of Vessel 2 (5303), c. Vessel 3 (sn).

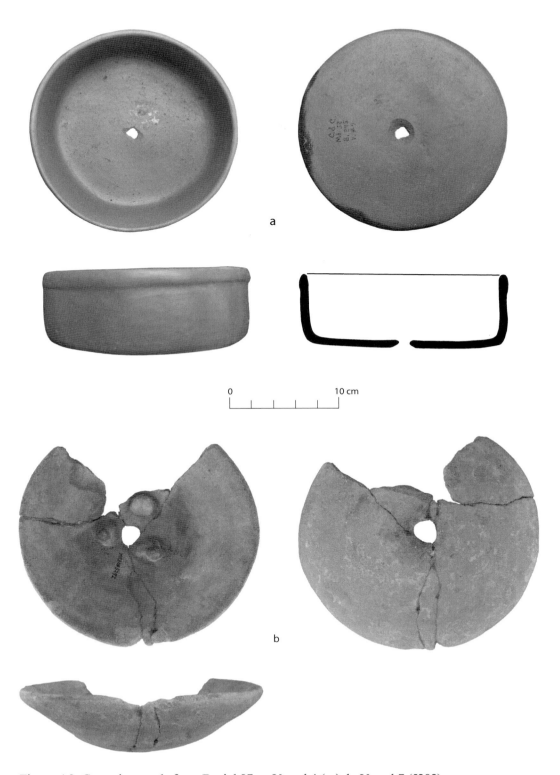

Figure A2. Ceramic vessels from Burial 87; a. Vessel 4 (sn), b. Vessel 7 (5292).

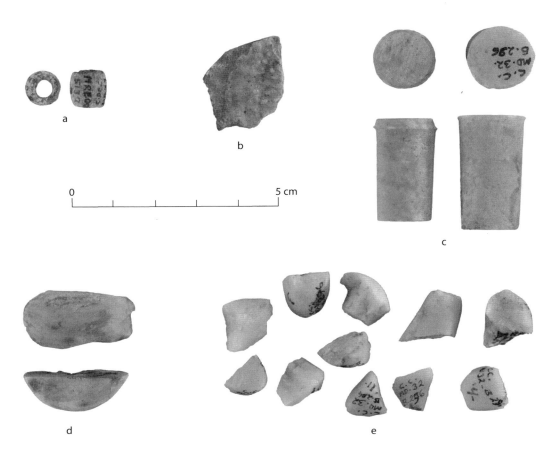

Figure A3. Artifacts from Burials 87 and 88; a. bead from Burial 87 (5232-2), b. fragment of shell ornament from Burial 88 (sn), c. travertine drill cores from Burial 88 (sn), d. white quartz pebble from Burial 88 (sn), e. fragments of white quartz pebbles from Burial 88 (5165).

the excavation. We are positive that the vessel described here came from Burial 295, and it was the only vessel from there that was in one piece. The "4" of this vessel could have been a misread of a "9" recorded in the field (or the other vessel could have had the illegible number). We cannot resolve this mixup on the basis of notes or photographs. It is ironic that the excavators would have lost track of their most pristine vessel, but the fact that special care was taken with it may have been the reason it became lost. If it were separated from the others early on, it would not have been at hand for later study. We have encountered this irony many times in working with artifacts from previous excavations. Artifacts accorded special care are

more frequently lost and forgotten than those treated in bulk.

Vessel 1 (5304): The plaster patches on this rim fragment indicate this vessel was restored. The rim fragment shown in Figure A1a (also, Figure 11) was probably meant for the NWAF type collection. The vessel had a slightly beveled outturned rim on a vertical neck. The exterior diameter of the thickened rim is 24.0 cm. The vessel wall is 1.2 cm thick. It is of fine orange paste and has a thin, light gray carbon core. The well-smoothed and burnished surface is light yellowish brown (5YR 6/4 light reddish brown). There are traces of light red paint on a stucco surface on the outside of the pot (10R 6/4 pale red).

Vessel 2 (5303): This is our best guess as to the particular vessel represented by the partial rim fragment of this bowl of complex profile. The sherd also looks like a sample of a broken whole vessel for the type collection. This is of the Nambiyugua Smoothed type of Chiapa de Corzo with a smoothed surface but not slipped. It has medium coarse paste. There is no obvious wear on the rim. The vessel was 15.0 cm in outer diameter. It has a light brown surface (10YR 6/4 light yellowish brown) with some patches of fire clouding.

Vessel 3 (sn): Our attribution of this Mound 32 vessel to Burial 87 is also our best guess. It is slightly bigger (16.3 cm in outer diameter) than the sketch drawing of Vessel 3 (Figure 11) in the preceding report. This light brown vessel is of the Monte Rico Polished Brown type. It has some patches of fire-clouding. It is 6.0 cm high, 16.3 cm in diameter, weighs 350.6 g, and has a vessel volume or capacity of 750 ml. The walls are 1.6 cm thick. The vessel has a complex profile with a small, concave base that shows extensive abrasion wear on its prominent margins. The interior of the bowl also shows significant wear on the convex bottom. In contrast, there is almost no wear on the rim. There was a lot of calcium carbonate deposits on the interior of the bowl, an indication that it was mouth-up in the ground.

Vessel 4 (sn): The troubled pedigree of this pot was outlined above. It is a vertical-wall bowl of Sierra Red: Sierra Red Variety. It has a kill hole through its base that was drilled three-fourths of the way through the base from the exterior and then punched out the rest of the way. This break allowed us to test it for calcite temper, and it reacted positively to the test. We cannot definitively say that this vessel came from Burial 87, but that is the most plausible explanation of whatever labeling and inventory errors occurred. The photograph indicates that most of the pots from number 4 upward were found near the head of the burial. The kill hole in this pot would place it there. These pots are commonly found over the faces of burials. That the pot came from a burial is evident in the two small bags of human bone fragment still in the pot, many of them fragments of a human skull. If this pot is from this burial it would be the only known pot with a kill hole found in a tomb at Chiapa de Corzo (see Clark 2017). This bowl is the same red color (2.5YR 4/8 red) as the more common Mundet Red type (see Burial 297) and was only distinguished by its paste as an imported vessel from the Maya Lowlands. The vessel has slight bolstering on the exterior rim, forming a band just over a centimeter wide. It is 5.4 cm tall and has an exterior diameter of 15.2 cm. The exterior base is slightly convex and shows mild wear near the its center. There is also slight wear on the interior bottom of the vessel and on the rim. The vessel was obviously used before it was placed with the burial. The vessel had a capacity of 740 ml, or the size of a healthy single serving.

Vessel 7 (5292): Our attribution of this inner-horn burner bowl is also our best guess because the labels on the vessel are unclear. This vessel looks like it has ancient breaks (Figure A2b), and the burner bowl found with Burial 88 evident in the photograph (Figure 14) was clearly intact. The vessel of medium coarse paste is of the Copoyo Unslipped type of Chiapa de Corzo. It is 5.0 cm tall, with an exterior diameter of 18.6 cm, and with walls 9.4 mm thick. It is dark brown to black (10YR 7/2 light gray) because of burning on its interior and exterior. The three short, pointed horns around the hole through the bottom of the curved dish lean outward. This center hole appears to have been made after the vessel was fired – or at least widened through percussion removal. There are traces of white plaster on the exterior of the vessel. Other than burning, the vessels shows little evidence of wear from abrasion or much handling.

Jadeite Bead (5232-2): The excavators list two beads as Item 8. This spherical, light green, speckled jadeite bead is apparently one of this pair (Figure A3a). It is 9.2 mm long and 8.9 mm in diameter. It is biconically drilled, with an opening diameter of the hole of 4.0 mm.

Burial 88 (Figures A4-A6)

For the same reasons listed for Burial 87, we had to provide a new number to Burial 296; it became Burial 88 and Tomb 13 in the Chiapa de Corzo numbering system of burials and tombs. For this burial, Martínez and Lowe

list 14 ceramic vessels, a pair of small jade earspools, and 11 small pieces of quartzite as mortuary goods. We report and describe a few more objects and six of the vessels they mention (Figure A6a). Unlike the guess work for Burial 87, all but one of the vessels described here are secure and can be verified for this burial by comparison to those illustrated in Figure 15.

Vessel 2 (sn): Nambiyugua Smoothed bowl with complex profile; 6.5 cm high, 15.0 cm exterior diameter of the mouth, 7.2 mm thick, and a capacity of 600 ml. The bowl is light tan (5YR 6/4 light reddish brown) with black patches from fire clouds. It has a slightly concave base that shows mild wear on its salient edges (Figure A4a).

Vessel 4 (5277): Fragment of a complex profile bowl that we think is a fragment of Vessel 4. The vessel was 5.5 cm high with a mouth diameter of 13.0 cm. The walls are 6.7 mm thick. This bowl is an early version of Turi Coarse ware. It has been dusted with red pigment on both its exterior and interior surfaces. Unlike Vessel 2, this bowl has not been smoothed but has a roughly finished exterior. It has a gray exterior (5YR 4/1 dark gray) with orange-colored patches (7.5R 4/6 red). It had a concave base (Figure A4b).

Sherd disk lid (5251): This ceramic lid is shown in Figure 15 as being the lid to Vessel 8, but their differences in diameter make this impossible. The lid is 10.7 cm in diameter and 1.1 cm thick (Figure A4c). It appears to be made from a base sherd and is extremely flat and worn and has well dressed and ground edges. It may have been found inside of Vessel 8 but this vessel has an interior mouth diameter of 12.5 cm. As shown in Figure A4e, the lid is a perfect fit for Vessel 7, and this is the only vessel that it does fit. As shown in Figure 15, Vessel 7 was found resting on Vessel 8, so it would have been easy to confuse the two.

Vessel 7 (sn): Mirador Orange Vitreous jar with pronounced shoulder and flat base; 11.8 cm high, exterior rim diameter of 12.0 cm, wall thickness of 5.8 mm, and a vessel capacity of 1600 ml. It is of fine, temperless, hard-fired orange paste the same color as the matte orange surface of the rim and neck (2.5YR 5/8 red). A large band around the shoulder has orange

slip. The jar is not slipped. It has dark gray and black patches from fire clouding. The flat base is slightly concave and shows use. The rim also shows evidence of significant use (Figure A4d). As shown in Figure A4e, the sherd disk lid is a perfect fit for this jar.

Vessel 8 (sn): Flat-bottom vase of light yellow-orange, coarse paste; 12.8 cm tall, 14.5 cm mouth diameter, wall thickness of 1.2 mm, and vessel capacity of 1625 ml. The vessel has a thin white slip (5YR 8/1 white) on the exterior base and walls that slops over the interior rim (Figure A5a). It shows no evidence of abrasion from use. We could not match this vessel to any ceramic types in the NWAF collection for Chiapa de Corzo.

Vessel 11 (sn): Cueva Grande white-rim black bowl with outslanting sides; 5.7 cm high, 16.5 cm exterior mouth diameter, 4.9 mm thick, and capacity of 750 ml. The vessel is made of fine paste. The light rim is actually orange (Figures A5b and A6a). The main body of the vessel is black (2.5YR N3/ very dark gray). The transition zone between the orange rim and the black body is a thin band that is light tan in color. The color transitions have very clear margins rather than blurred. The exterior base shows extensive wear, and the interior base or bottom of the bowl shows mild wear.

Vessel 13 (sn): Mular White vase with a smudged band; 12.7 cm high, 13.5 cm mouth diameter, 4.5 mm wall thickness, 1500 ml vessel capacity. This fine paste elegant vessel is one of the more intriguing pots we have seen in a long time (Figure A5c). Its paste is brick red but its slip is black and whitish gray. Its color scheme is deceptively simple (Figure A6a) but must have required several firings to achieve the black base and black band just below the rim in an otherwise whitish exterior. The black band has diffuse margins and is flanked on both sides by thinner bands of orange and brown. It is black on the interior with one large white splotch. Its exterior is covered with red hematite paint, and this is also on the interior from the lip about 3 cm down. The vase evinces heavy wear on its exterior base at its edges but only mild wear on its rim and interior base. Most of the calcium deposits on this vessel were on the inside,

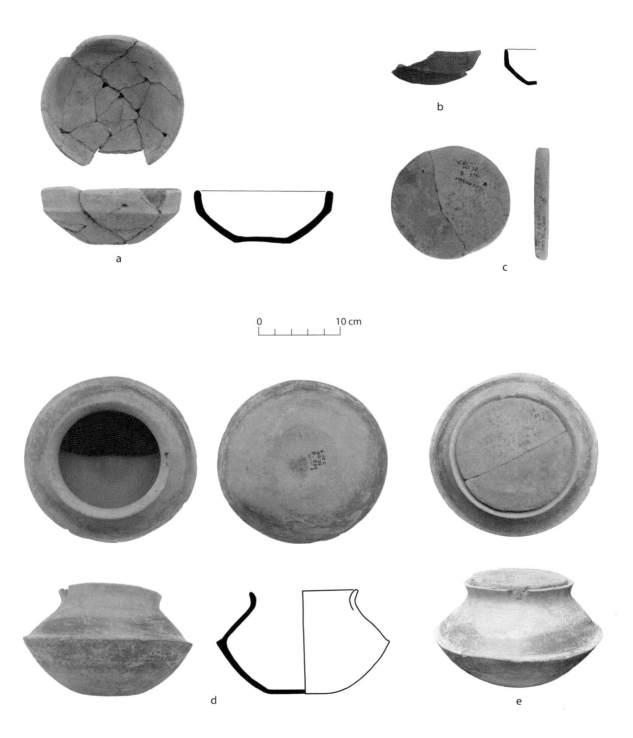

Figure A4. Ceramic vessels from Burial 88; a. Vessel 2 (sn), b. rim fragment of Vessel 4 (5277), c. sherd disk lid for Vessel 7 (5251), d. Vessel 7 (sn), e. Vessel 7 with its lid.

0   10 cm

Figure A5. Ceramic vessels from Burial 88; a. Vessel 8 (sn), b. Vessel 11 (sn), c. Vessel 13 (sn).

indicative that it was oriented mouth-up in the grave (see Figure 15).

Jar (5273); Large sherd from a jar attributed to this burial in the artifact forms. It lacks a rim but had a sharp shoulder junction. The vessel diameter at the shoulder is 14.0 cm, and the walls are 7.0 mm thick (Figure A12a). The vessel is slipped dark brownish gray (10YR 5/1 gray). It had a flat base.

Shell ornament (sn): Fragment of a thin piece of river clam shell with one worked margin; 2.6 cm long, 1.8 cm wide, and 2.5 mm thick (Figure A3b). It may have been part of an ornament.

Travertine drill cores (sn): These two travertine drill cores are unusual in that the faces of their wide ends have been ground smooth (Figure A3c). The shorter core is 2.4 cm high and 13.6 mm in diameter. The other core is 2.7 cm high and 14.5 mm in diameter. It is possible that they were part of the earware of the buried individual rather than manufacturing waste. The fact that they were found in the tomb, and that no other examples of drill cores were found in the general excavations suggests that these items were more than manufacturing waste. The pair of jade earspools found with Burial 88 are described as "small." If the scale drawing of them is accurate, they were 4.0 to 4.5 cm in diameter with throats 1.5 cm wide. These throat openings would have been big enough to insert the drill cores as center pieces as types of earplugs.

White quartz pebble (sn): This is half of an elongated pebble of milky white quartz; 2.5 cm long, 1.4 cm wide, and 9.4 mm thick (Figure A3d). None of the fragments of quartz described below came from this pebble. It is about ten times the size of the small chunks found in the group of 11 pieces near the waist of the burial.

Eleven white quartz pebble fragments (5165) were found in the pelvic area of the individual interred in this tomb (Figure A3e). The excavators comment that these were fragments of broken pebbles rather than whole pebbles. We were able to refit 3 chunks of opaque white quartz into three-fourths of an original pebble. The other fragments are more angular and of translucent quartz. They come from at least two different pebbles, with one

piece representing one pebble. It is not clear whether the pebbles were broken to obtain the correct number of pieces or whether there was additional significance. Martínez and Lowe suggest that these pebbles were contained in a bag. Similar speculation was advanced for Burial 253 of Mound 15 for the 11 small, white quartz pebbles found in the pelvic area (Glauner et al. 2017). This burial dates to the following Horcones phase and indicates continuity in this unusual practice. As noted, another piece of a larger pebble was found with Burial 88, apparently apart from the others.

Burial 297 (Figures A6b-A11)

The mortuary offering of this burial is the most complete. Unfortunately, the excavators did not record or describe the burial's precise location, other than to say that it was not in the central patio with the two tombs recovered in Mound 32. Of the 11 vessels they list with the burial, we describe 10 of them. These are illustrated in color in Figure A6b to show the lack of variety of colors and the stark contrast between the large red bowls and the small black or dark brown plates and dishes. We include large sherds of two half bowls listed in the artifact records as also coming from this burial. We would not be surprised if these bowls were burial offerings broken in the process of finding the burial with a backhoe. They are not mentioned in the report of the burial. The two largest vessels are missing large sections of their rims and look like they were cut through with the same stroke of a backhoe claw (Figure A6b). If true, their matching breakage patterns would indicate that these two vessels (1 and 5) had been in a lip-to-lip arrangement (Figure A9). The field photograph and labels are not clear on this point, but this appears to be a plausible interpretation. The two vessels we add to the artifact inventory may also have been cut through during excavation.

Vessel 1 (5264): Mundet Red plate with grooved wide-everted rim; 7.7 cm high, 44.5 cm exterior rim diameter, 1.2 cm thick, vessel capacity of 5650 ml, and it weighs over 2600 g. With the missing portion it may have weighed 3000 g. One fourth of the rim of this vessel is missing from severe excavation damage that

a

b

Figure A6. Ceramic vessels from burials; a. Vessels from Burial 88, b. Vessels from Burial 297.

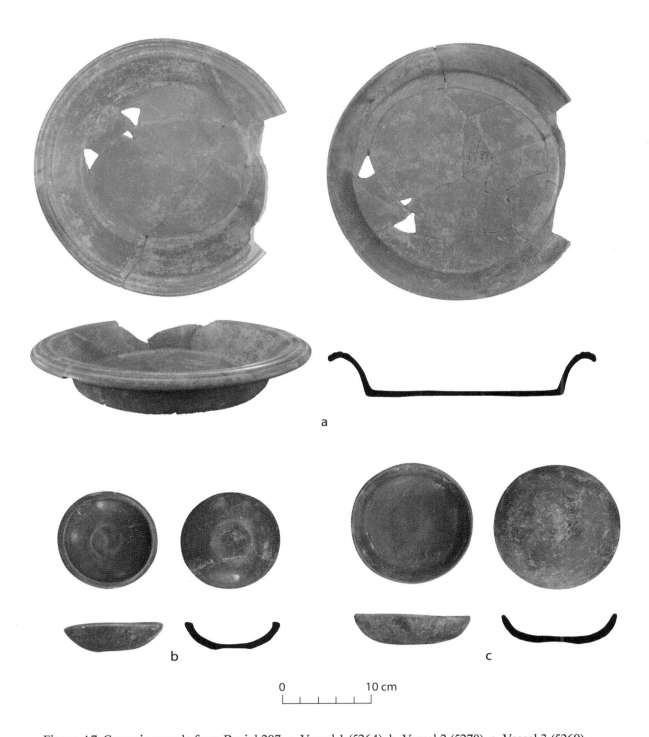

Figure A7. Ceramic vessels from Burial 297; a. Vessel 1 (5264), b. Vessel 2 (5270), c. Vessel 3 (5269).

probably involved the backhoe (Figures A6b and A7a). This would explain why the broken parts of this vessel were not recovered. This vessel has dark orange paste with white specks of ash temper and a thick, smooth red slip (2.5YR 5/6 red) on all surfaces. The exterior base is slightly concave. It shows moderate abrasion wear on edges of the exterior base. Most of the calcium deposits we cleaned from this vessel were on its interior, indicating that the vessel was mouth-up in the excavation. This position is supported by the field photograph (Figure 16).

Vessel 2 (5270): Monte Rico Brown bowl with a concave base; 4.0 cm high, 12.7 exterior rim diameter, 9.0 mm wall thickness, and 200 ml vessel capacity. Chips through the thick, dark brown to black (5YR 3/2 dark reddish brown) slip on the rim reveal an orange paste beneath. There is no evidence of abrasive wear on the rim or interior, but there is on the edge of the slightly concave base (Figure A7b).

Vessel 3 (5269): Monte Rico Brown dish (5YR 3/1 very dark gray); 4.3 cm high, 15.7 cm exterior rim diameter, 9.2 mm wall thickness, capacity 400 ml. This thick, sturdy dish has the same mouth diameter as Vessel 11. It has a slightly concave base but shows no evidence of wear. There is a black residue in this vessel from something having been burned in it. It is very black and has left a crackled, scaley slip. Perhaps this bowl served as a censer. The other burials had interior-horn burner bowls (Figure A7c).

Vessel 4 (5267): Monte Rico Brown jar (2.5YR N3/ very dark gray) with complex shoulder and pre-slip grooved design of chained triangles; 10.0 cm high, 8.1 exterior rim diameter, 5.2 mm wall thickness, vessel capacity 750 ml. There is no evidence of use. The vessel appears to have been pristine when placed in this burial. The sharp shoulder juncture of this jar is like that of the Mirador Orange Vitreous vessel found with Burial 88. A chip from the rim (excavation damage) reveals a dark gray paste (Figure A8a).

Vessel 5 (5276): Nicapa Orange basin (2.5YR 5/8 red) with light yellow paste with a thin light gray carbon core; 12.7 cm high, 35.5 cm exterior rim diameter, 9.7 mm wall thickness, capacity 6750 mm. Very few temper

particles are evident in the paste. This vessel shows extensive wear on its exterior base but very little on its rim or interior (Fig A8b). It is slightly worn on the sharp juncture where the rim turns inward. The lack of interior wear indicates that it was not some sort of stirring bowl. As proposed above, we think this vessel was placed mouth down on Vessel 1 in a lip-to-lip arrangement. This positioning would explain the complementary damage pattern seen on both (Figures A7a and A8b). The excavators do not mention this positioning, and the one photograph (Figure 16) is inconclusive. One implication of our hypothesis is that both vessels were whole before the salvage crew found them at the base of the mound. The vessel is now missing a third of its wall. Most of the calcareous deposits on this vessel were on its exterior, indicating that it was placed in the grave upside-down, a position commensurate with the pattern of excavation damage. Our identification of this vessel as Nicapa Orange resist ware presents a chronological problem because this type is typical of Chiapa III times, and Burial 297 appears clearly to date to Chiapa V times. Vessel 5 has light splotches on its interior and exterior that look like Nicapa resist rather than wear through the orange paste to the slip. There is no good evidence that manufacture of this type continued past the Chiapa III or Escalera phase. This vessel is a good candidate for an heirloom pot. If so, it remained in remarkably good shape for two or three centuries. Another point of interest, Vessels 5 and 1 look as if they were made for each other. They make a very nice set, as shown in the drawing of them in a lip-to-lip arrangement (Figure A9). If Vessel 5 is significantly older than its matching plate, this would imply that the plate was made to fit it.

Vessel 6 (5275): Betania Red-rim White jar; 7.0 cm high, 5.5 cm rim diameter, 5.8 mm wall thickness, capacity 120 m. This vessel is one of a pair of small jars (Figures A6b and A10a). It has a rounded base free from wear, but there are chips from its rim, perhaps from use. It is slipped on the exterior of the entire vessel and inside on the rim. It is not slipped below the rim on the interior. The body is white (5YR 2/1 white) with three oval daubs of slip on the

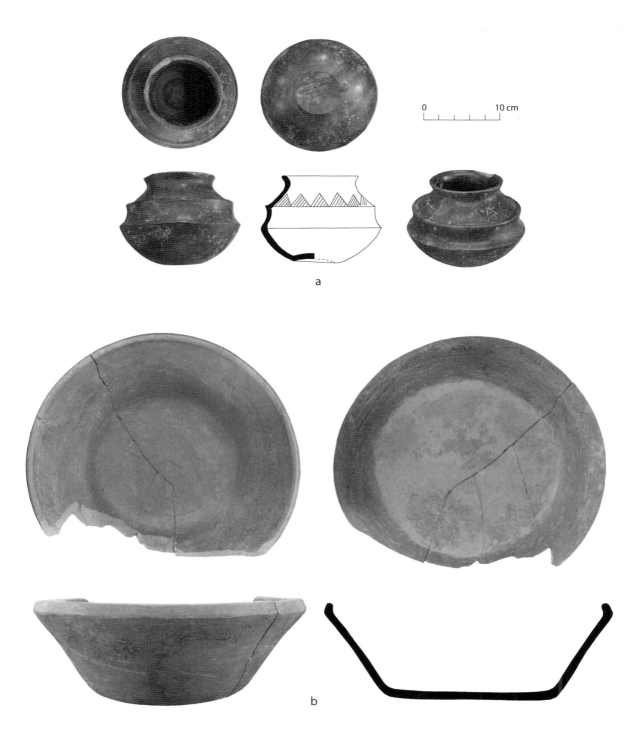

Figure A8. Ceramic vessels from Burial 297; a. Vessel 4 (5267), b. Vessel 5 (5276).

Figure A9. Vessel 1 and Vessel 5 from Burial 297 in a lip-to-lip arrangement.

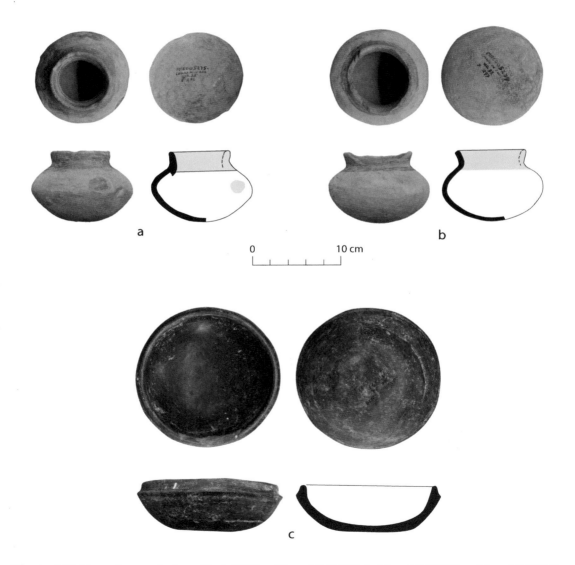

Figure A10. Ceramic vessels from Burial 297; a. Vessel 6 (5275), b. Vessel 7 (5274), c. Vessel 8 (5271).

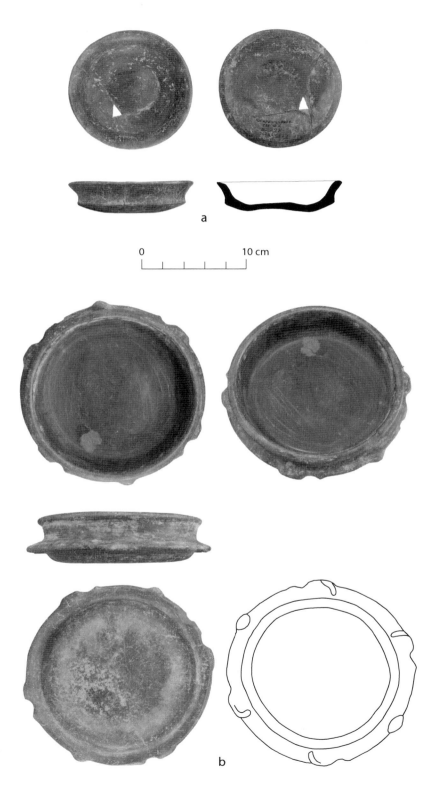

Figure A11. Ceramic vessels from Burial 297; a. Vessel 10 (5272), b. Vessel 11 (5268).

shoulder the same orange-red color as the rim (5YR 5/8 yellowish red).

Vessel 7 (5274): This small jar is the same type and color scheme as Vessel 6, but it lacks the three daubs of paint on its shoulder juncture (Figure A10b). This jar is larger and better made than its mate; 7.3 cm high, 6.6 cm rim diameter, 5.1 mm wall diameter, capacity 150 ml. This jar also has a chipped rim from use but no obvious wear on its exterior base. These chips reveal a medium-fine orange paste with sparse ash particles as temper.

Vessel 8 (5271): Monte Rico Brown dish (5YR 4/3) with an exterior ridge just below the rim; 4.4 cm high, 13.3 cm exterior rim diameter, 6.7 mm wall thickness, 260 ml capacity. This vessel has a dark orange paste with fine ash temper. It shows no evidence of wear. Most of the calcium deposits from water percolating through the soil for centuries were on the outside of this vessel, indicating that it was bottom-up in the burial, perhaps as a lid for another vessel (Fig A10c).

Vessel 10 (5272): Monte Rico Brown dish (5YR 4/4 reddish brown); 2.8 cm high, 11.7 cm exterior rim diameter, 5.3 mm wall thickness, 125 ml vessel capacity. The slip on this vessel is variegated and ranges from black to splotches of orange-brown (Figure A11a). A chip through the thick, burnish slip reveals orange paste. The vessel shows no signs of use-wear. There were extensive calcium deposits from soil salts on the interior of this vessel, indicating that it was face-up in the grave. Its diameter matches perfectly that of Vessel 8. It is possible that this vessel was in a lip-to-lip arrangement with Vessel 8.

Vessel 11 (5268): Monte Rico Brown bowl (5YR 3/2 dark reddish brown) with everted and notched medial flange; 4.2 cm high, 15.7 cm exterior rim diameter, 8.8 mm wall thickness, 600 ml vessel capacity. This vessel has the same rim diameter as Vessel 3 and could have served as a lid to that vessel in a lip-to-lip arrangement. Vessel 11 is slipped on all its surfaces. Its flat base is slightly concave and shows moderate wear on its rim. There is a chip missing from the interior base (Figures A5b and A11b) that was caused by a pick hitting its exterior base, thus the vessel was upside down in the grave. Most of the calcium deposits are also on the exterior,

indicating this position in the soil for centuries. The missing chip on the vessel interior reveals an orange paste. There is no wear on the inside or on the rim. The medial flange is actually a representation of animal with a small face, tail, and four appendages, all equally spaced to divide the circle of the bowl in six equal pizza slices. Martínez and Lowe describe this vessel as having a faint negative design of parallel lines and probably being a type of Usulatan pottery imported into the site. We could find no evidence of such a design on this pot or any of the others from this burial. This description caused great difficulty in matching the burial pots to their descriptions. The bowl shown in Figure 16 as Vessel 9 appears to show an interior design. This vessel was not available for examination, and we can find no description of it. We presume this is the vessel with the negative resist design and likely an imported pot.

Red bowl (5265): This Mundet Red bowl (2.5YR 5/6 red) is represented by two large fragments that are not conjoining pieces (Figure A12b). This flat-bottom bowl with outturned rim was 7.4 cm high with an exterior diameter of 31.0 cm and a wall thickness of 8.5 mm. A large fragment of a red plate with the two rim sherds appears to be from a different vessel of nearly the same size.

Red bowl (5266): This Mundet Red bowl (2.5YR 4/8 red) is of the same form as that just described, but much smaller (Figure A12c). It is 4.5 cm high, 21.0 cm in diameter, and with a wall thickness of 8.9 cm. It was a sturdy little bowl. The MRE records indicate this vessel and the previous one came from Burial 297, but they are not reported as such. They may have been considered as sherds rather than vessels, but they clearly were part of whole vessels broken in excavation.

Cache 32-1

Martínez and Lowe do not report any caches from their excavations. We propose the existence of at least one as a logical necessity to explain the whole bowl found in general excavations. As evident in their report, their excavations were harried and difficult, conditions not conducive to the most thorough

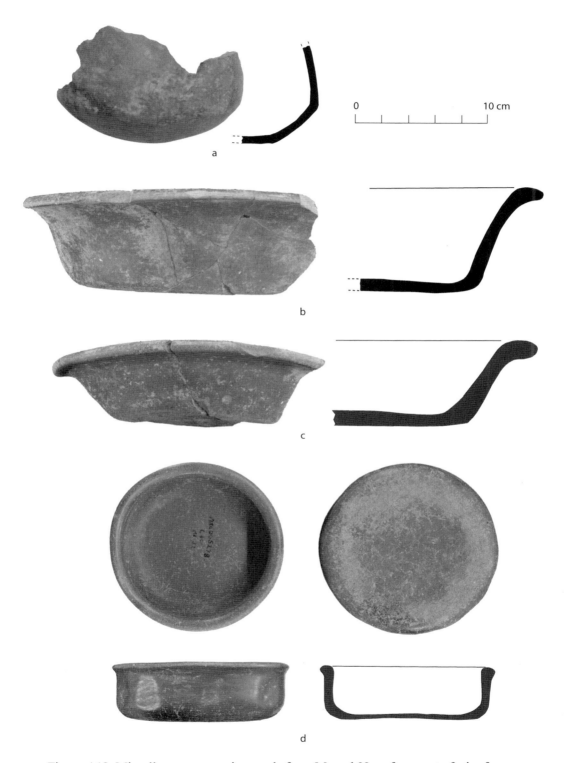

Figure A12. Miscellaneous ceramic vessels from Mound 32; a. fragment of a jar from Burial 88 (5273), b. Mundet Red bowl from Burial 297 (5265), c. Mundet Red bowl from Burial 297 (5266), d. Mundet Red bowl from Cache 32-1 (5278).

documentation of finds—as apparent in the incomplete descriptions of mortuary furniture noted above. We doubt the excavators saw the precise context of the whole bowl we report here, thus they recorded it as a random find in general excavations.

Red bowl (5278): This flat-bottom, vertical wall bowl appears to be a Sierra Red vessel and probable import. It is 4.2 cm high, 12.5 cm in diameter and with walls 8.8 mm thick and a vessel capacity of 260 ml. Nine flat facets were impressed around the bowl's exterior just above the base (Fig A12d). The base is slightly concave, thus all the abrasion wear is on the outer perimeter. The wear is heavy on the exterior base but light on the edge of the rim and in the interior of the vessel. There were significant deposits of calcium in the vessel interior, an indication that it was placed face-up in its offering or burial.

CERAMIC ARTIFACTS

In this section we describe the rest of the artifacts made of fired clay found in the Mound 32 excavations. The bulk of them are figurine fragments. Most of these repeat types were reported by Thomas Lee (1969) for the site. We devote more description to the few figurine fragments that are not represented in his report. Lee focused on formal properties, and these sort out well chronologically for some types, but his system mixes figurines from significantly different time periods. We are more interested in the time period and have looked more at the composition of the paste and some decorative techniques as being more sensitive to time.

Many of the artifacts we illustrate here are illustrated in the report, but we provide a different set of photographs and more views. Clark also redrew the designs of the ceramic stamps. He devoted more time to reconstructing broken parts of stamps that are evident in the cut marks at the base of previous designs. The drawings illustrated in the body of this report

(Figure 32) deal with features that are still salient and that can be picked up from making rubbings of the stamps. The drawings we propose attempt to capture more detail, many of them indicated by dashed lines in Figure 32.

Red-on-Cream Sherds (Figure A13)

These are sherds found in general excavations illustrated in this report with a drawing (Figure 30). We include a color photograph of them here because Lowe (1995) placed special emphasis on sherds of this type in his interpretation of the ethnic identity of the Guanacaste phase peoples who resided at Chiapa de Corzo. He was impressed ever since his excavations at Mound 1 in 1955 that sherds from fancy vessels of this type imported from the Maya Lowland were found in fill but never as whole vessels in the numerous caches and burials found at the site (see discussion in Glauner et al. 2017). In his opinion, more sherds of this type, and larger sherds as well, have been found at Chiapa de Corzo than found in the land of their origin, supposedly somewhere in the Maya Lowlands. Their frequency at Chiapa de Corzo, and apparent pedestrian use and discard, presents a paradox that he thought indicated a prohibition in their usage, as mentioned in the preceding report. The color photograph better conveys the elegance of this pottery. The most elaborate decorated sherd illustrated in Figure A13 somehow was left off the original illustration (cf. Figure 30).

Human Figurines (Figures A14-A22)

Our treatment of fragments of human figurines follows the format and categories described by Lee (1969) for Chiapa de Corzo. Remarkably, some of the figurines illustrated here were not represented in his much larger sample of figurines from the site. This may be because prior to the excavation of Mounds 15 and 32 few excavations at this site encountered Guanacaste phase deposits.[1] Lee's typology has

---

[1] Another factor could have been theft of figurines found. Lee told Clark on several occasions a story that a local resident would come to the ceramic lab in Tuxtla Gutiérrez with her very young son and engage Bruce Warren in conversation to distract him while her boy stole figurine heads from the baskets lining the base of the wall. These were apparently sold from their gas station. They were eventually found out and the loss halted, but who knows how many figurine heads got away, and of what types.

Figure A13. Red-on-cream sherds.

subtleties that are hard to follow. We are more interested in the original ages of these figurines and less in his typology. Most of the fragments of human figurines predate the construction of Mound 32 and are presumably from fill material nearby and thus indicative of earlier occupation in this sector of Chiapa de Corzo.

Preclassic Heads:

Early Olmec style figurine (5064): This is the earliest figurine known for Chiapa de Corzo and dates to the Cotorra phase. It is in the style of San Lorenzo, Veracruz, for the San Lorenzo phase. It has an elongated, narrow head and slit eyes (Figure A14a). This figurine is made of medium-fine orange paste (7.5YR 6/4 light brown) and may be locally made rather than being an import from the Gulf Coast region. The head is 3.1 cm high, 1.7 cm wide, and 1.5 cm thick. Of course, it could have been brought in from some place closer, such as Mirador or San Isidro, both of which had occupations of this period.

Early Olmec style figurine (5066): This is a face fragment of a larger early Olmec figurine made of fine tan paste (10YR 6/4 light yellowish brown) with a thick gray core (5YR 5/2 reddish gray). The fragment is 4.6 cm high from chin

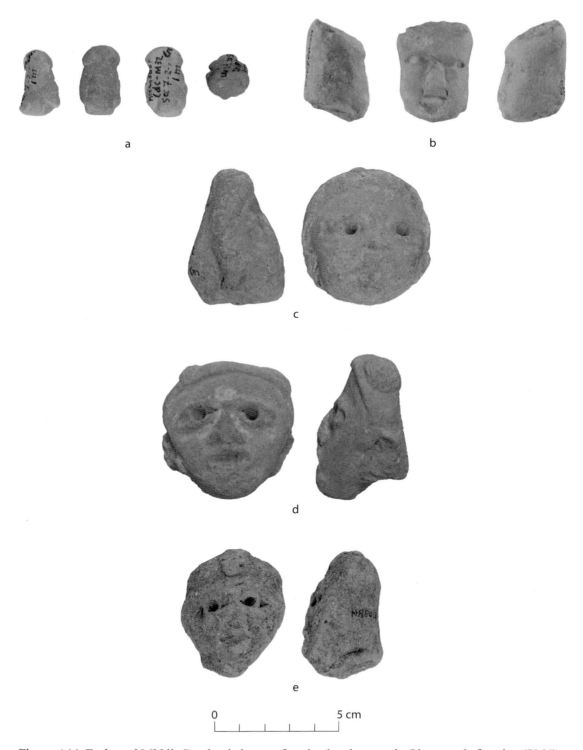

Figure A14. Early and Middle Preclassic human figurine heads; a. early Olmec style figurine (5064), b. early Olmec style figurine (5066), c. Type I-Chiapa-A4 (5075), d. Type I-Chiapa-A9 (5074), e. Type I-Chiapa-A2 (5069).

Figure A15. Middle Preclassic human figurine heads; a. Type I-Chiapa-B1 (5065), b. Type III-Chiapa-A (4902), c. Type III-Chiapa-A (5068), d. Type III-Chiapa-A (5067), e. Type III-Chiapa-A (5931), f. undesignated type (5070).

to crown, 3.2 cm wide at the forehead, and 2.7 cm thick. This figurine has more open eyes than Specimen 5064 (Figure A14b). Its ears and hair ornament have been broken off. There are traces of red paint on its forehead and back of the head. This figurine fragment could be an import from the Gulf Coast region.

Type I-Chiapa-A4 (5075): This is the type of figurine popular in Chiapa II times. Compared to the Early Olmec style, these figurine heads were round face and have pyramidal shapes in side view, expanding from a small crown to a very wide neck (Figure A14c). They have large punched irises. They are made of coarse paste. This figurine is 5.9 cm high, 5.3 cm wide, and 3.9 cm thick at the neck. It is of a light orange paste (5YR 6/3 light reddish brown). Its topknot has been broken off (cf. Lee 1969: fig. 2p).

Type I-Chiapa-A9 (5074): This figurine has a triangular rather than round face. The hair decorations are still preserved. It is of medium coarse, hard-fired orange paste (5YR 6/2 pinkish gray). It is 5.9 cm high, 5.3 cm wide at the top of the cheeks, and 3.6 cm wide at the neck (Figure A14d). It appears to have had earspools. This figurine was originally slipped white. Traces of this slip are apparent under the eyes and along the base of the nose (cf. Lee 1969: fig. 3m).

Type I-Chiapa-A2 (5069): This figurine head is highly eroded and its variety is less certain. Its eyes are characteristic of early Middle Preclassic figurines. It is 5.3 cm tall, 4.2 cm wide at the ears, and 3.2 cm thick at the level of the nose. It is of coarse orange paste (10YR 5/3 brown). Its hair is arranged in a Mohawk.

Type I-Chiapa-B1 (5065): Heavily eroded figurine fragment missing the lower part of the face, but the eyes with fine punctated irises are still visible (Figure A15a). It is made of medium-fine yellow paste (10YR 7/4 very pale brown). It is 3.4 cm high, 2.7 cm wide, and 2.2 cm thick. Of all the figurines, this looks most like the Middle Preclassic figurines from La Venta, Tabasco (cf. Lee 1969: fig. 4i).

Type III-Chiapa-A (4902): This fat-cheek figurine head sports a fancy hair piece and small earplugs (Figure A15b). It is very similar to a figurine illustrated by Lee (1969: fig. 8b). This specimen is made of medium-fine yellow paste (7.5YR 6/4 light brown) with a dark gray carbon core. It is 4.0 cm high, 4.2 cm wide, and 3.4 cm thick. It was originally slipped white; small patches of slip are evident on the face and in the crevasses for the eyes.

Type III-Chiapa-A (5068): This fragment is a rare find of a head attached to a torso (Figure A15c). It is of made of medium-fine dark brown paste (10YR 5/2 grayish brown). Tresses run down each side of the face to large disks on the ears. The figurine also has a round pendant on the chest. It is 5.5 cm high, 4.4 cm wide, and 2.8 cm thick at the lower face (cf. Lee 1969: fig. 9a).

Type III-Chiapa-A (5067): This figurine head is broken at the forehead but its lower face is intact. It is of medium-fine, brick red paste (5YR 5/6 yellowish red), a color which could result from this figurine having been burned.

Type III-Chiapa-A (5931): This figurine head fragment has the distinction of having been made into a tool associated with drilling with a bow drill. It is made from medium-fine yellow paste (7.5YR 5/0 gray). The back of the head is gone, and in is place is a deep cavity made by a solid drill (Figure A15e). The rotary wear is very apparent in this cupped depression. The head fragment is the same size and shape as the small sherd disks with drilled cavities found in abundance at Mound 15 (see Glauner et al. 2017) which are thought to have been used as cap pieces for bow drills. This fragment is 3.4 cm high, 3.4 cm wide, and 1.9 cm thick (cf. Lee 1969: fig. 9c).

Undesignated type (5070): Figurines with this unusual variant of a coffee-bean eye have not been reported for Chiapa de Corzo (Lee 1969), Mirador (Agrinier 2000), or La Libertad (Miller 2014), the three Preclassic sites in Chiapas with the most human figurines. This figurine appears to be Middle Preclassic and is closest in appearance to Redonda style figurines from Mirador (see Agrinier 2000: fig. 71a), but there are significant differences in the presentation of the eyes. This figurine head from Mound 32 is the most complete found in the excavations. It is of medium-fine, dark reddish brown paste (7.5YR 3/0 very dark gray) and has a burnished face. The hairdo is elaborate, and the size of the complete nose is impressive. The head is 4.7 cm high, 4.0 cm wide, and 3.6 cm thick from the tip of the nose to the back of

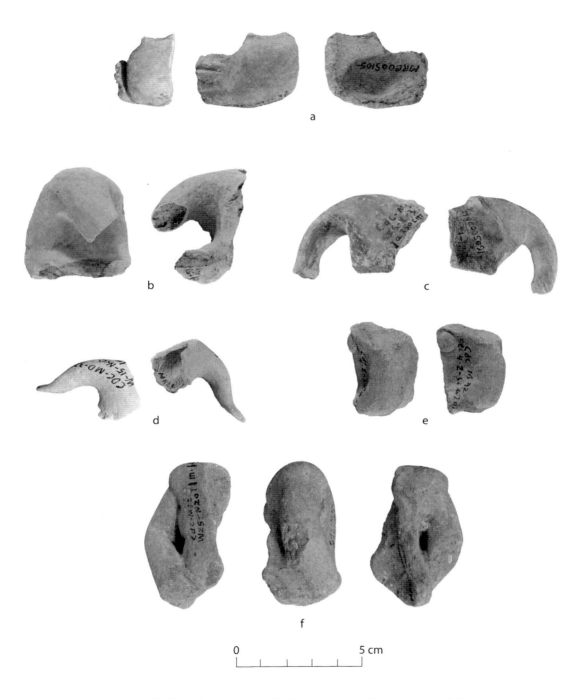

Figure A16. Fragments of hollow figurines; a. left cheek and mouth of face (5105), b. right arm and fragment of torso (5091-2), c. left arm and torso fragment (5091-1), d. left arm and hand (5091-3), e. left arm and torso fragment (5090-2), f. right arm and torso fragment (5090-1).

the head. The face has a naturalistic appearance as if it could be a depiction of an actual person (Figure A15f).

Hollow Figurines:

Left cheek and mouth of face (5105): This is a quarter fragment of a face of a burnished figurine of medium-fine reddish brown paste (10YR 7/2 light gray). It is 3.2 cm high, 4.4 cm wide, and 14 cm thick (Figure A16a). The full face would have been about 6 cm wide and 8 cm high.

Right arm and torso fragment (5091-2): this is a fragment of a seated figurine. It is of fine white paste (10YR 7/3 very pale brown) with a dark gray carbon core (7.5YR 4/0 dark gray), as most evident in the break of the solid arm (Figure A16b). The fragment is 4.2 cm high and 3.4 cm wide. It has a carefully smoothed and burnished surface.

Right arm and torso fragment (5091-1): This is the fragment of a hollow upper torso attached to a solid arm (Figure A16c). A very slight breast is indicated, and this provided the orientation of this piece. It is made of dark brown fine paste (7.5 YR 5/2 brown) and is burnished. It is probably a fragment of a male figurine. It is 3.9 cm high and 5.0 cm wide from the elbow to the center of the torso.

Left arm and hand (5091-3): The designation of this figurine fragment is a bit ambiguous. It is made of fine, light orange paste (7.5YR 8/2 pinkish white) on the outside that fired dark gray on the inside. The bottom of the flipper-like hand is gray and has evidence of a break, so it was attached to something (Figure A16d). The fragment is 2.5 cm high and 4.4 cm long along the arm.

Left arm and torso fragment (5090-2): This figurine fragment is of coarser paste than the preceding. It is smoothed but not burnished. It is probably from a Preclassic figurine and earlier than the fragments described above. It portrays a left arm and the front of a torso showing a disk-shaped ornament around the neck (Figure A16e). It is made of medium-fine reddish brown paste (5YR 5/4 and 5/3 reddish brown). It may have been slipped. It is 3.6 cm high and 2.4 cm wide.

Right arm and torso fragment (5090-1): This figurine fragment is made of medium-fine yellowish orange paste (7.5YR 6/4 light brown). It is nearly a solid figurine and only has evidence of a small hollow in the torso. It has traces of pinkish white slip on the surface (10YR 6/3 pale brown). This appears to be a fragment of a Middle Preclassic figurine. The right hand is on the belly. The figurine is depicted as wearing some sort of shawl-like garment over the shoulder (Figure A15f). This fragment is 5.9 cm high, 3.5 cm wide, and 2.8 cm thick.

Preclassic Torsos:

Male torso (5086): This the most complete and best preserved human torso found at Mound 32. It is made of medium fine, hard fired pale paste (10YR 7/2 light gray). The figurine still has a yellowish white slip, and traces of red paint are evident behind the knee joint and in the neck area. The figurine wears a perforated, circular ornament around the neck and also has a triangular pubic covering (Figure A17a). It has a flat back, straight waist, flat and squared breasts, all indicative of a male. The figurine was standing but the legs indicate a dynamic pose, with the bent knee. The navel has been crudely dug out, making the cavity bigger. This fragment is 8.4 cm high from knee to shoulder, 5.3 cm wide at the broken arms, and 2.7 thick from the slightly rounded belly to the back. The full figurine would have been about 16-18 cm tall.

Female torso (5085): This torso fragment is of coarse reddish orange paste (7.5 YR 5/4 brown) with lots of ash temper. The figurine has a dark carbon core, most evident on the tenon that once connected the torso to the legs. This figurine is of a female, as evident in the pronounced waist constriction and the crudely made protruding, rounded breasts (Figure A17b). It also has a very large navel. The figurine fragment is 5.4 cm high, 5.5 cm wide at the broken arms, and 2.9 cm from the tips of the breasts to the flat back.

Female torso (5083): This torso is of light tan paste (7.5YR 6/4 light brown). It was burnished light yellowish brown rather than being slipped. It is broken at the head and waist. It has a slight constricted waist, and the breasts were prominent, with the nipples indicated by punctation. The breasts have been broken off

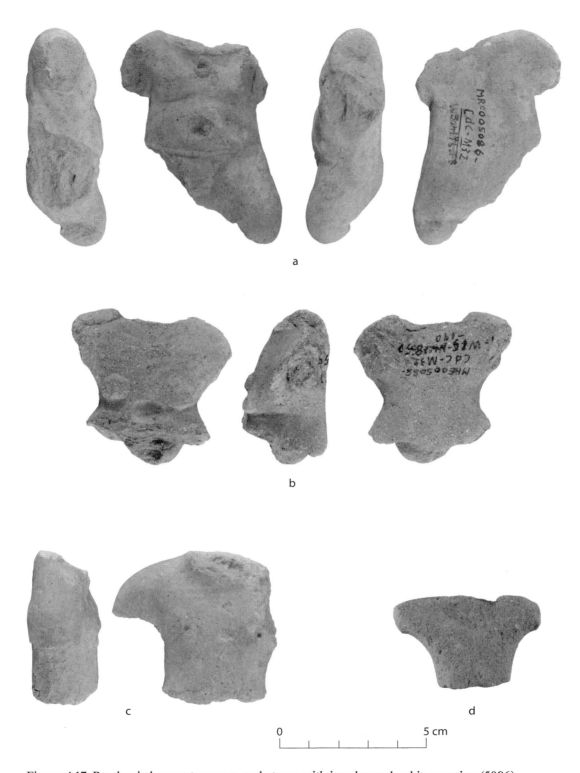

Figure A17. Preclassic human torsos; a. male torso with jewelry and pubic covering (5086),
b. female torso (5085), c. torso with punctated breasts (5083), d. female torso (5084).

(Figure A17c). We think it likely portrayed a female. The fragment is 5.7 cm high and 6.1 cm wide, and 2.5 cm thick from the breasts to the back.

Female torso (5084): This figurine fragment is highly eroded, and its remaining features are more difficult to appreciate in the photographs. It is of brick red medium-fine paste and has a dark core. The current color is probably the result of having been burned. Indications of breasts are rather low on the torso, near the lower break. These are heavily eroded but they appear to have represented female breasts. The ends of the broken arms are completely rounded off. The neck break is particularly interesting because it indicates that the head was in a forward position rather than upright (Figure A17d). The fragment is 3.5 cm high and 5.4 cm wide. (7.5YR 6/4 light brown)

Female torso with upper arm (5087): This torso is highly eroded but still clearly indicates a female with constricted waist and swollen belly. The arm is broken off at the elbow. It is of coarse, dark brown paste (5YR 3/2 dark reddish brown) with ash temper. It is 3.8 cm high and 4.1 cm wide (Figure A18a).

Female torso (5095): This torso fragment has a particularly interesting feature. It is broken down the middle and shows the root of the head that was attached by this tenon (Figure A18b). The torso was clearly built around the already formed head. This figurine has a very pronounced breast and is clearly female. It is made of medium-fine reddish brown paste (5YR 4/2 dark reddish gray) with ash temper. The fragment is 4.8 cm high and 4.3 cm wide.

Fragment of seated figurine (5097-1): This figurine is made of medium-fine orange paste (5YR 5/6 yellowish red). It is yellowish brown on the interior. The upper right leg is attached to the torso of this seated figurine. It had a slight curved back. The leg was bent at the knee, so the figurine was seated tailor fashion (Figure A18c). The navel is depicted as a horizontal opening. There is also a trace of a pubic covering. The fragment is 6.0 cm high and 3.3 cm thick at the waist.

Fragment of lower torso of seated figurine (5097-2): This figurine fragment is of medium-fine light orange paste (5YR 6/4 light reddish brown) but lacks a carbon core. This figurine also has a horizontal navel and flat buttocks (Figure A18d). It is 3.8 cm high and 3.5 cm wide at the level of the navel.

Fragment of standing figurine (5096): This figurine was slipped white and still retains much of its slip. It is a fragment of the left hip. This depicts a triangle in the pubic area (Figure A18e). The figurine has a constricted waist and slightly curved back. It probably is from a female figurine. It is of medium-fine light orange paste (10YR 7/4 very pale brown). It is 6.4 cm tall, 4.6 cm wide, and 3.6 cm thick.

Arm and hand with long fingers (5104): This figurine was made of dark brown, medium coarse paste (7.5YR 4/2 dark brown). It is burnished. The fragment is of a left arm bent at the elbow and a long hand on the belly. The thumb of the hand has been broken off (Figure A18f). Just above its former position there is an indication of a large navel. The torso of this figurine was slightly hollow.

Limbs of Preclassic Figurines:

Upper left leg of seated figurine (5103-1): This is a fragment of a white-slipped, seated figurine of medium-fine orange paste (5YR 6/4 light reddish brown). An incised line on top of the thigh goes underneath and is an indication of a skirt (Figure A19a). This portion of the figurine was left unslipped as a yellowish orange garment; only the lower half of the upper leg is slipped. The leg is broken off at the knee but indicates that the figurine was seated tailor fashion. The leg is 7.5 cm long and 3.7 cm wide at the groin.

Fragment of upper left leg of seated figurine (5103-2): This leg fragment is of coarse orange paste with ash temper (7.5YR 5/4 brown). The end of a bent knee is visible. The leg is 5.2 cm long and 3.0 cm wide (Figure A19b).

Fragment of upper right leg of seated figurine (5103-3): This figurine has the same paste and reddish coloring as 5103-2 (5YR 6/6 reddish yellow) but is not from the same figurine. The leg is shorter and squatter. It is 4.8 cm long and 3.2 cm wide (Figure A19c).

Right foot of hollow, seated figurine (5101-1): This is a fragment of a large figurine made of medium-fine, light orange paste (5YR

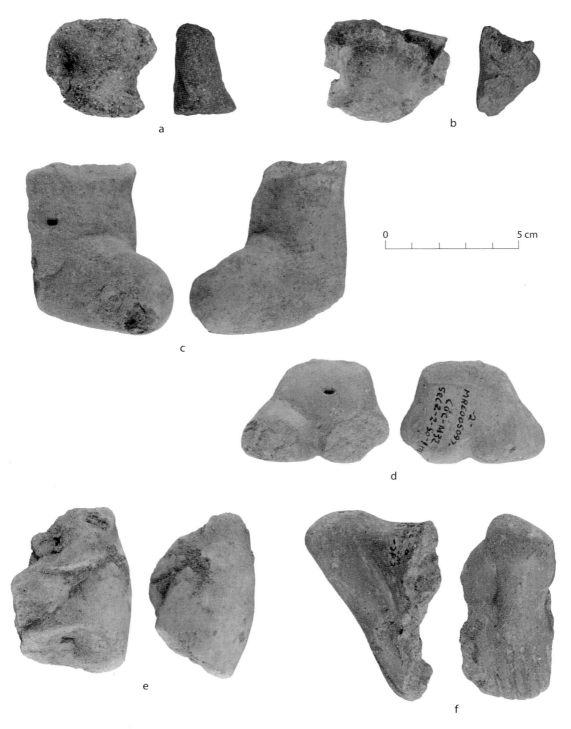

Figure A18. Preclassic human torsos; a. female torso with arms (5087), b. torso of fat or pregnant female (5095), c. fragment of seated figurine with torso and upper left leg (5097-1), d. fragment of lower torso and buttocks of seated figurine (5097-2), e. fragment of standing figurine with bent knees (5096), f. arm and hand with long fingers (5104).

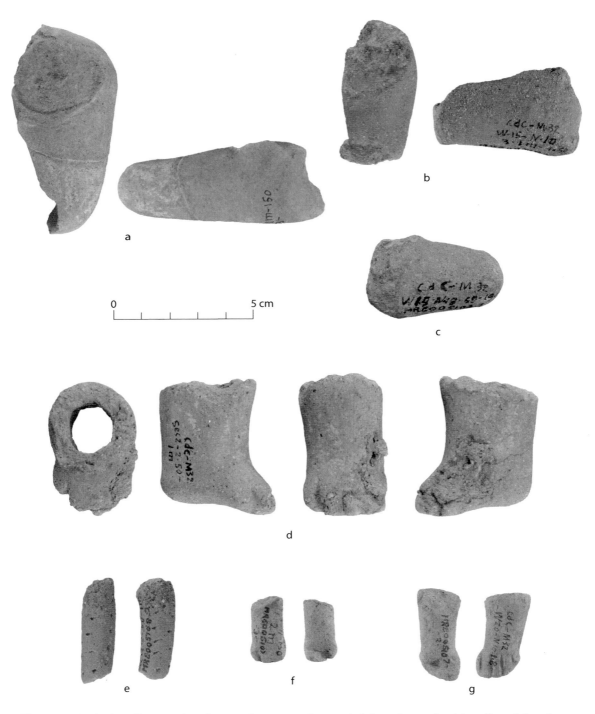

Figure A19. Limbs of human figurines; a. fragment of upper left leg of seated, white-slipped figurine with a skirt (5103-1), b. fragment of upper left leg of seated figurine (5103-2), c. fragment of upper right leg of seated figurine (5103-3), d. foot of hollow figurine, probably seated (5101-1), arm fragment with punctation (5108-2), f. left hand in a semi-fist (5107-3), g. left hand (5107-2).

6/4 light reddish brown). Its surface is smoothed but not burnished. There are tiny traces of white slip. Five toes are indicated (Figure A19d). The bottom of the foot is arched from toes to heel. The top of the foot has evidence that something was broken from this area, probably the hand of the figurine. The fragment is 5.0 cm long, 3.6 cm wide at the top of the leg fragment, and 3.0 cm thick.

Arm fragment with punctation (5108-2): This is the shaft portion of a straight limb that could be from an animal or a human wearing clothing. It is of medium-fine, brownish gray paste (10YR 5/2 grayish brown). The small punctations are vertical on one side of the limb and horizontal on the other side (Figure A19e). It is 4.2 cm long and 1.4 cm in diameter.

Left hand (5107-3): This hand and forearm fragment is of medium-fine, yellowish gray paste (10YR 7/2 light gray). It depicts a left hand with cupped fingers and a well-defined thumb in a semi-fist position (Figure A19f). Some of the fingers are broken off. Traces of red pigment are visible in the palm of the hand. This figurine was probably slipped. The fragment is 2.6 cm long and 1.3 in diameter.

Left hand (5107-2): The hand of this fragment is not as well-defined as that for Specimen 5107-3. This fragment is of medium-fine to fine yellow paste (10YR 7/4 very pale brown). The thumb is not clearly defined, but the arc defined by the extended fingers indicates this is a left hand (Figure A19g). This arm and hand fragment probably came from a slipped figurine. The forearm and hand fragment is 3.4 cm long and 1.6 cm wide at the elbow.

Later Figurine Heads:

Type III-Chiapa-A (5072): This is a well-preserved figurine head of hard, medium-fine, light orange paste (5YR 7/4 pink) that was hard fired. Very few temper particles are evident. It bears no trace of erosion, and other than missing the tip of the nose knocked off during excavation, it has a pristine surface. The surface was smoothed but not burnished, thus it has a rustic look and feel. A headband frames long hair down the back and a long, half-bang over the left eye (Figure A20a). The figurine sports a pair of large disks on its ears. It is similar to a figurine illustrated by Lee (1969: fig. 9c). The break at the neck reveals an interesting feature. It shows the head was built around a long, conical projection or tenon rising from the body. This is the reverse of the technique for Middle Preclassic figurines in which the tenon is an extension of the head, and the body is attached to it (see Figure A18b). The head is 5.1 cm tall, 5.7 cm wide at the ear ornaments and 3.7 cm thick from the tip of the broken nose to the back of the head. Lee (1969:32) lists this type of figurine as dating to the Francesa-Guanacaste phases.

Type III-Chiapa-A (5071): This is just a fragment of a lower face. It is of the same paste and of similar coloring (10YR 6/4 light yellowish brown) as Specimen 5072. It has the same style of eyes, but eyebrows are deeply cut into the forehead rather than incised or modeled (Figure A20b). The mouth is more open, and upper teeth are defined with the same sort of cutting. The tip of the nose has been broken off. It is similar to figurines illustrated by Lee (1969: fig. 9). This face fragment is 4.2 cm high, 4.3 cm wide at the cheeks, and 3.8 cm thick from the nose to the back of the head.

Undesignated type (5073): The face outline and head shape of this figurine are unlike any illustrated by Lee (1969) for Chiapa de Corzo. The large extended ears and rectangular shape of the head remind one of the famous sculpture from the Huastec area. These flat ears have earspool ornaments clearly indicated (Figure A20c). These are the only details remaining of this face. The face of this figurine appears to have been deliberately broken off. All that remains are traces of thick plaster. Perhaps the ceramic face was removed and replaced with one modeled in plaster. There is no indication of hair or any other decoration other than the earspools. This figurine is made from a different kind of paste and may have been imported into Chiapa de Corzo. The paste is fine textured and varies from light orange (on the back) to grayish tan (on the front) (10YR 6/2 light brownish gray). It has a carbon core. It is 5.6 cm high, 5.7 cm wide at the earspools, and 2.4 cm thick at the middle of the destroyed face.

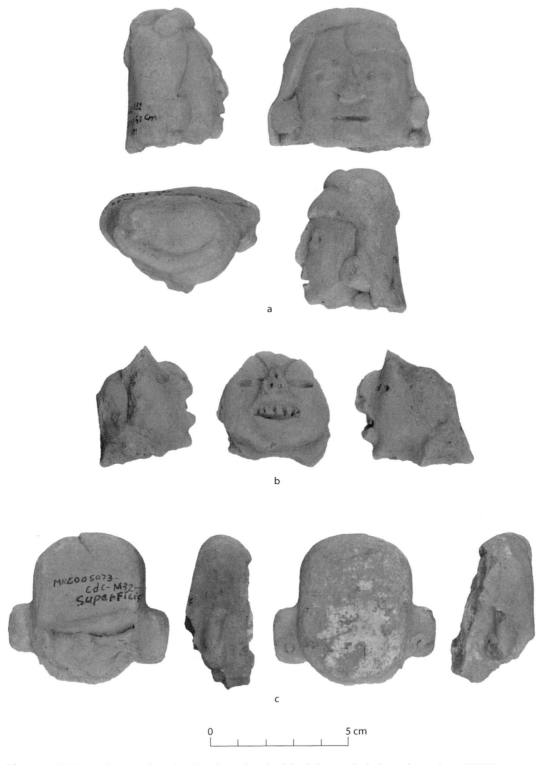

Figure A20. Later human figurine heads; a. head with elaborate hairdo and earplugs (5072), b. lower face (5071), c. head with a destroyed face (5073).

Fragments of Later Human Figurines:

Torso and right arm of hollow figurine (5088): This hollow torso fragment is of medium-fine, light orange paste (5YR 6/4 light reddish brown) with few aplastic inclusions. It is smoothed, but not burnished. The attached solid right arm is broken just above the elbow. Three circular elements indicate a necklace of some kind (Figure A21a). These irregular circles were cut into the figurine and are not impressions from a hollow tool such as a reed or bird bone. This fragment is 5.5 cm high and 3.4 cm wide.

Right torso and arm of hollow figurine (5089-1): The right arm of this hollow, seated figurine is attached to the body rather than being free from it as with Specimen 5088. The four-fingered hand rests on the belly. A pronounced breast is evident above the crook of the elbow, indicating a female figurine. It is made of medium-fine orange paste (5YR 5/3 reddish brown) and has been carefully smoothed but not burnished (Figure A21b). It is similar to Type III-Chiapa-A figurines illustrated by Lee (1969: fig. 7l, m). The fragment is 5.7 cm high and 3.8 cm thick at the leg.

Right torso and arm of hollow figurine (5089-2): This figurine fragment is similar in concept to that just described but is significantly smaller. It is of similar medium-fine orange paste (5YR 6/3 light reddish brown) and has a smoothed but unburnished surface. Its four-finger hand rests on the abdomen. The fingers are crudely indicated by three impressions. Two oval, appliqué beads of a necklace are evident just below the neck, and there is a scar where another bead has broken off (Figure A21c). There are no clear markers of secondary sexual characteristics. This figurine is similar to two of the III-Chiapa-A type illustrated by Lee (1969: fig. 7l, m). This fragment is 3.7 cm high and 3.4 cm wide.

Left leg of seated figurine (5102): This figurine is of a different paste and temper recipe than the rest. It has coarse orange paste (7.5YR 6/4 light brown) tempered with angular fragments of crushed limestone. It is crudely made and not smoothed. It is not clear whether this is an arm or a leg, or of a human or an animal. Our best guess is that it is the right leg of a seated figurine, with knees drawn up close to the body rather than in tailor fashion (Figure A21d). The bottom of the foot is flat and would fit this interpretation. Crude grooving indicates four digits. There is also a grooved incision just above this at the level of the ankle. The leg is 4.6 cm high from the base to the top of the knee.

Limb with digits (5107-1): This limb fragment could be of an arm or a leg. The digits are crudely indicated with three short impressions (Figure A21e). It is broken just above the slightly flexed knee or elbow. It is made of hard, fine to medium-fine pinkish orange paste (5YR 6/3 light reddish brown). It is 5.3 cm long and 1.8 cm in diameter.

Left leg with foot (5101-2): This lower leg fragment is of medium-fine orange paste (5YR 6/3 light reddish brown). It is probably from a seated figurine, with legs in tailor fashion. The bottom of the foot is arched (Figure A21f). The toes have been broken off. The fragments 4.6 cm long, 2.4 cm wide, and 2.3 cm thick.

Effigy Fragments:

Head fragment (5077): The difficulty in understanding this complicated fragment of a hollow effigy leads us to believe that it is all the more important to attempt the task. We are not sure which end is up. We illustrate it here as if the long extension at its unbroken end was a beard rather than a headdress. The rim of a circular eye socket is evident on the left of the fragment (viewer's perspective) (Figure A22a). We interpret the narrow, projecting part at the upper part of this fragment as some sort of nose, but the lack of nostrils makes this a difficult interpretation. Between the raised central element and the possible beard are appliquéd bands that look like a mouth, and just above this is a possible mustache. This fragment and the others in Figure A22 are of the same medium-fine orange paste (5YR 6/3 light reddish brown, 5/6 yellowish red) evident in the Type III-Chiapa-A figurines described above, hence we have grouped these items together because we think they are of the same paste group and contemporaneous. These same figurines and effigy fragments have designs made by cutting with a thin sharp tool and other designs commonly attributed to punching with reeds. The circular, punched designs shown on

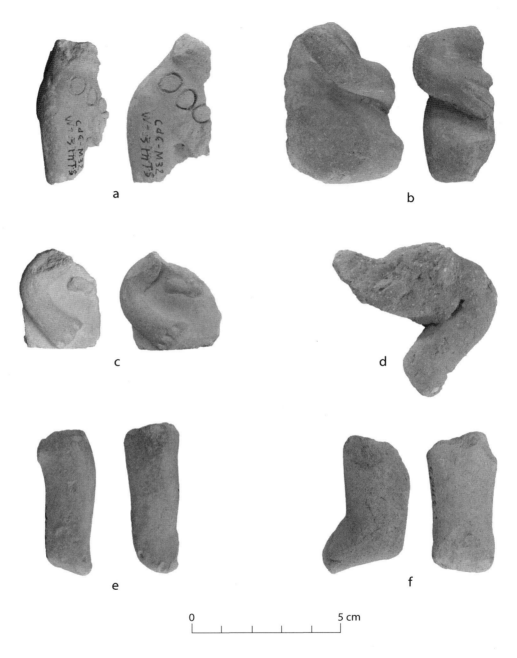

Figure A21. Fragments of later human figurines; a. fragment of torso and right arm of hollow figurine (5088), b. hollow figurine fragment of right torso and arm on belly (5089-1), c. fragment of right torso and right arm of hollow figurine (5089-2), d. left leg of seated figurine (5102), e. right leg with foot and toes (5107-1), f. left leg with foot (5101-2).

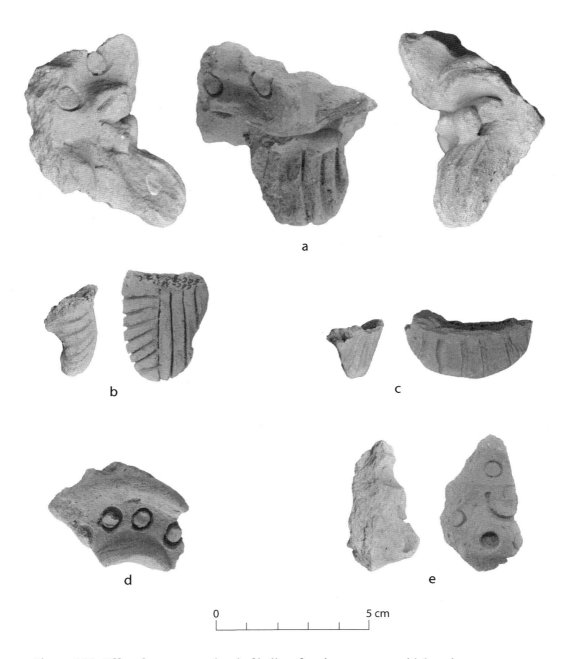

Figure A22. Effigy fragments; a. head of hollow figurine or censer with beard or headdress element (5077), b. beard or headdress element (5094-1), c. beard or headdress element (5094-2), d. eye element of hollow figurine or censer (5115-3), e. unidentified element (5115-1).

specimens in Figure A20 may have been made with bird bone rather than reeds. Two impressed circles are evident on this fragment on the side of the nose and just below the eye – if we have oriented it correctly. Alternatively, they would have been decorative elements above the eye. This fragment is 5.9 cm high and 5.0 cm wide.

Beard or headdress element (5094-1): This fragment is of the same color (5YR 6/6 reddish yellow) and paste as the effigy fragment just described, and it is of the same form as the element we interpret as a beard. But the slashed design in this fragment splits it down the middle into vertical and horizontal features, something that would be difficult for a beard but not unusual for a headdress element (Figure A22b). This piece is 4.8 cm long and 3.5 cm wide.

Beard or headdress element (5094-2): This is another appliqué element that was only loosely bonded to its figurine. It has the same cut design and general form as the beard or headdress element of Specimen 5077, but the cut marks appear to have been made with a sharp stick rather than a stone flake (Figure A22c). The fragment is of similar paste and color (5YR 6/4 light reddish brown). None of these pieces have been burnished, rather they have rough, rustic exteriors. This piece is 2.7 cm long and 4.9 cm wide.

Eye element of hollow figurine or censer (5115-3): This fragment looks like a fragment of an eye socket. It has evidence of four impressed circles (Figure A22d). We have oriented this as the upper rim of the eye rather than the lower one. It is of the same paste and coloring as Specimen 5077. This piece is 3.5 cm high and 4.6 cm wide.

Unidentified element (5115-1): The paste of this piece, and the impressed circle decoration on it indicate this was from the same sorts of effigies as the other pieces (Figure A22e). We do not know what this is from.

Animal Figurines (Figures A23-A25)

Based on their paste composition, some of these figurine fragments appear to be from objects that may have been made in the Protoclassic period. Others are of coarse paste that corresponds to the pastes used in Middle and Late Preclassic times and thus are as old as most of the human figurines. The range of animals represented is limited compared to those found at the contemporaneous Mound 15 (Glauner et al. 2017); all of them appear to represent mammals or birds. We do not see anything that looks reptilian or amphibian. The most frequent figurines are of canids and birds.

Dogs:

Head (5079): This is the most elaborate figurine head found in the Mound 32 excavations. It is made of fine orange paste. The exterior of this figurine varies from light to dark brown (7.5YR 6/2 pinkish gray). The eyebrows and mouth were made with deep cuts, as seen on some of the III-Chiapa-A figurines (see Figure A20b) and likely dates to the same time; other features have been impressed. The head is broken off at the neck just below a lateral suspension hole that was made when the clay was still wet. Two vertical groves provide detail to the rounded, vertical ears (Figure A23a). The eyes were made of small balls of clay with small center punctations (cf. Lee 1969: fig. 28n). Two small holes were impressed at the end of the snout to define the nose. Red pigment is evident around the eyes and along the snout. Random small linear impressions on each side of the head appear to indicate fur. On the right side of the snout is a flat element with two long grooves that, at first glance looks like a lolling tongue, but it is probably the end of a paw at the side of the face. The head is 3.8 cm long from the tip of the nose to the back of the head and 3.5 cm wide between the ear tips.

Head and torso (5081): This canine figurine is more complete than that just described but of more generic representation. It is of coarse reddish orange to brown paste (7.5YR 6/4 light brown) with numerous small black crystals. It is the forward half of the dog. The body was long and flat. The front legs have been broken off at the shoulders (Figure A23b). The eyes are deeply punched and are placed almost in the base of its vertical, triangular ears. It has a pointed nose but no nostrils. The paste and style of this figurine looks Middle Preclassic. It is 5.0 cm long from nose to its broken hindquarters, 4.4 cm tall, and 3.4 cm wide.

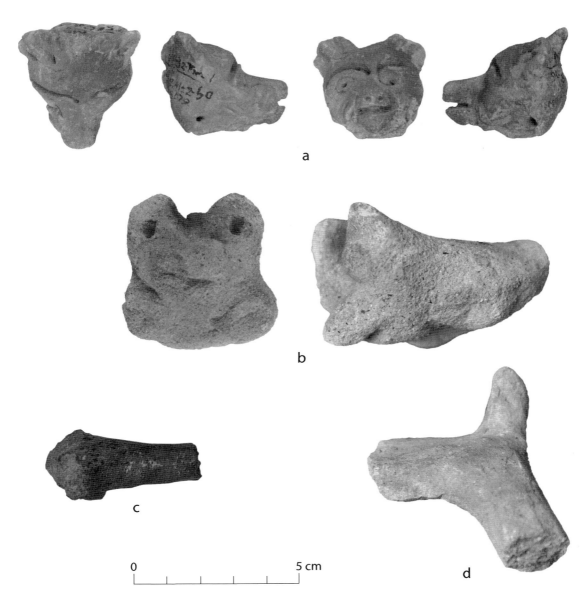

Figure A23. Dog figurines; a. dog head with incised detail (5079), b. fragment of dog with generic head, torso, and broken front legs (5081), c. forward torso of a dog (5093), d. rearward torso with back legs and upright tail (5092).

Front torso (5093): This artifact appears to be a dog torso similar to that just described. It is long, flat, and wide. The head is broken off at the neck and the front legs broken at the shoulders (Figure A23c). It is of medium-fine blackish paste (2.5YR 4/0 dark gray). It is 4.8 cm long and 3.5 cm wide.

Rear torso (5092): The hindquarters and happy tail of a dog with a tabular body are represented by this artifact. It is of medium-fine, light orange paste (10YR 6/3 pale brown). It is roughly shaped and not smoothed. Both of the back legs are broken off at the knees (Figure A23d). It is 8.3 cm long and 4.3 cm wide.

Rabbits:

Head fragment (5080-1): This hollow head fragment may have been an appliqué on an effigy vessel. It is of fine to medium-fine dark gray paste (7.5YR 4/0 dark gray). It is well smoothed and appears to have been burnished. The upright ears are well preserved as is much of the creature's right eye (Figure A24a). The eye is depicted as a bulging hemisphere. A wide shallow groove above the eye defines an eyebrow. This object is very hard fired and is of unusual paste. It could be from an imported vessel. It is 4.7 cm tall, 4.8 cm long, and 3.5 cm wide.

Head fragment (5080-2): This pair of rabbit ears is similar to those just described, but they come from a different hollow object or vessel (Figure A24c). They are of yellowish paste (10YR 6/3 pale brown), and the surface of the piece is slipped and burnished a tan to orange color. This was probably part of an imported effigy vessel. This figurine fragment is 3.6 cm tall and 3.1 cm wide.

Deer:

Head (5078): This hollow head fragment is of fine gray paste with a slipped and burnished gray surface, both which are characteristic of pottery from Oaxaca. This head was probably part of an effigy pot imported from there. The details on the head are realistic (Figure A24b). The head is broken off in front of the ears. The nose is broad and indicates the nostrils The eyes protrude and are outlined with shallow, broad grooves, an idea evident with the rabbit head (Figure A24a). This deer head fragment measures 4.5 cm from nose to the back of the head. It is 3.9 cm wide and 3.6 cm high.

Miscellaneous:

Mammal foot (5106): This object is of medium-coarse orange paste (7.5YR 5/2 brown). It appears to be a toed foot of a large animal figurine. The foot is broad and flat and thus does not look like a representation of a human foot. It is 4.8 cm long and 3.8 cm wide (Figure A24d).

Birds:

Pointed beak of a raptorial bird (5082): This is the beak of a very large bird. It is made of coarse reddish orange paste (2.5YR 4/4 reddish brown) with numerous small white particles of temper that look like a mix of sand and ash. The beak is broken from the head (Figure A25a). It is slipped matte red (10R 4/6 red) on the sides but not on the under surface. It is smoothed and burnished on the upper side of the beak but not the underside. The mouth is well-defined as are the nostrils in the beak. The paste is characteristic of Middle Preclassic wares. This appears to have been a large figurine or effigy. The beak is 6.3 cm long and 5.8 cm high.

Broad beak of aquatic bird (5119): This bird beak is as large as the one just described and is also separated from its head. The beak is broad and rounded, more like that of aquatic birds (Figure A25b). It is made of the same reddish orange paste (2.5YR 5/4 reddish brown) as that just described. The bird figurines or effigies these fragments came from must have been contemporaneous. The lower rims of open, circular or oval eyes are evident just above the beak and its well-defined nostrils. These are similar to the eyes of the unidentified effigy figurine (Figure A22a). There is no evidence that this figurine was slipped, but the top of the beak is reddish orange and the underside of the beak is yellowish (5YR 6/4 light reddish brown). Ancient artisans appear to have fired this figurine in a way to achieve this coloring. It is not smoothed or burnished. The beak is 5.9 cm long and 7.8 cm wide.

Broad bird beak (5114-1): This artifact is from another wide beak bird. It is of medium-fine orange paste (7.5YR 5/4 brown) and a dark reddish gray exterior (7.5YR 5/0 gray). It is not smoothed or slipped. This fragment appears to have been an appliqué on a pot rather than a figurine. A large disk is shown in the middle of the beak (Figure A25c). It is 5.0 cm long and 4.1 cm wide.

Eye fragment (5116-2): This fragment of a hollow figurine or effigy is the partial rim of an open eye (Figure A25d) such as those evident on Specimen 5119. We cannot verify, of course, that it came from a bird effigy, but the missing fragments of these bird heads would have fragments like this. This object is of medium orange paste (7.5YT 6/4 light brown). It is 4.8 cm long and 4.5 cm wide.

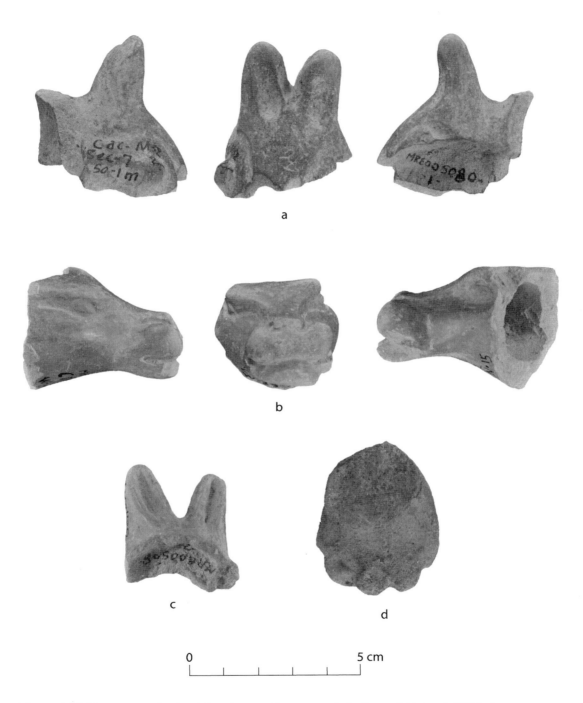

Figure A24. Fragments of animal figurines; a. fragment of a hollow rabbit head (5080-1),
b. hollow deer head (5078) c. fragment of a rabbit head (5080-2), d. solid foot of mammal (5106).

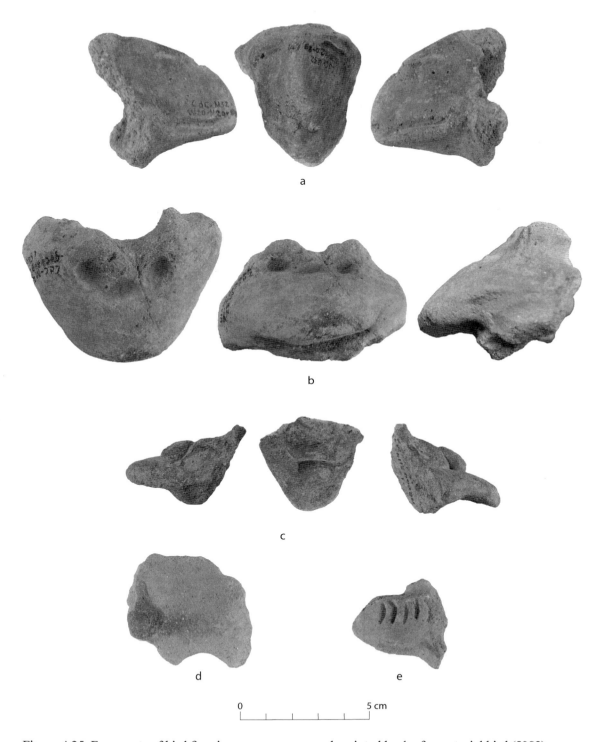

0   5 cm

Figure A25. Fragments of bird figurines or censers; a. red, pointed beak of a raptorial bird (5082), b. red, broad beak of aquatic bird (5119), c. broad bird beak (5114-1), d. fragment of eye of hollow figurine or censer (5116-2), e. fragment of eye and eyebrow of hollow figurine or censer (5114-4).

Eye fragment (5114-4). This fragment also is of the rim of an open, circular eye. It appears to have had a an eyebrow made of vertical elements similar to the flaming eyebrow of Olmec fame (Figure A25e). This is the upper edge of the piece. A piece of topknot is evident above the eyebrow. These objects could actually have been part of small masks rather than parts of large figurines or effigies. We lack the edge pieces to decide the matter. This object is also of medium, light brown paste (10YR 6/2 light brownish gray). It is 3.8 cm long and 3.9 cm wide.

Cylindrical Stamps (Figure A26)

Semi-solid stamp (5249): This object is listed as a cylindrical stamp but may not be. It is of medium-coarse orange paste (10YR 6/2 light brownish gray) and has a small cylindrical hole in the broken end. This may be a cavity created by building this object around a small stick which burned out in firing. The hole only goes in a centimeter. The design of two crossed bands and a floral element is repeated twice (Figure A26a). This cylinder is 7.3 cm long and 3.3 cm in maximum diameter. The design appears to be complete, which would suggest that only a small portion was broken off. The cavity in the cylinder, however, suggests that this object was probably twice as long and thus not a stamp in any ordinary sense. It could have been a decorated handle, but we know of no such objects. It has an elevated roll-out design. It is worth noting that the concept of this object differed from the rest of the stamps illustrated here. The design was made by adding clay elements to a prepared cylinder. For the other cylinder stamps the hollow clay cylinder was created to the proper thickness, and then the design was created by cutting away background to leave the elevated design.

Hollow stamp with double merlon icon (5122): This is the largest and most complete of the cylinder stamps. It is made of very fine orange-brown paste (10YR 6/2 light brownish gray) and has a very carefully smoothed surface and flattened ends. The stamp is 5 cm in diameter with walls 1.2 cm thick, leaving a throat opening of about 2.5 cm. The inside throat is rough. The curvature of the stamp represents about one-fourth of the original circumference. The wide band of the stamp was probably a central element. The design appears iconic, with a framed double merlon. The design looks like it was constructed with mirror symmetry. If so, the design would have repeated itself twice in a normal layout and measured 16.0 by 6.4 cm (Figure A26b).

Hollow stamp with geometric design (5123-2): This stamp is also made of very fine, light orange-to-tan paste (10YR 6/4 light yellowish brown). It is 2.0 cm in diameter and has walls 5.1 mm thick. The pattern on the preserved fragment is of triangles and chevrons. We think that the chevrons were the middle part of the design and that the missing edge was also of chained triangles. If so, the stamp would have been 3.8 cm wide. The diameter of the stamp would allow nine triangles on each side and nine chevrons in the middle (Figure A26c)

Hollow stamp with arm and hand (5123-1): This stamp had an anthropomorphic or zoomorphic design, depending on the owner of the arm represented. This is a rare representation for stamps at Chiapa de Corzo (see Lee 1969:73-84). Fredrick Peterson illustrates a fragment of a cylinder stamp (1963:114, fig. 171c) that depicts a deer with this shape of arm. This stamp fragment from Mound 32 was made of fine, pinkish paste (7.5YR 6/2 pinkish gray). It depicts an arm flexed at the elbow and a backward hand. It is from a cylinder stamp 4.0 cm in diameter, thus this 2.8 cm long portion of the stamp is less than a fourth of its circumference. The walls of the stamp are 8.6 mm thick at the flat end. The interior of the throat is slightly rough.

Stemmed, Flat Stamps (Figures A27-A28)

Raptorial bird (5124): This stemmed stamp had a figure eight configuration rather than a rectangular one. It is made of fine yellow paste (2.5YR 5/4 reddish brown) and smoothed and burnished on its carved, flat face. Traces of red paint are evident on its edges and back. The design is deeply cut with vertical walls and crisp edges, both of which help in reconstructing design elements for some pieces that have broken off. They can be detected by the cut and fracture marks on the background surface

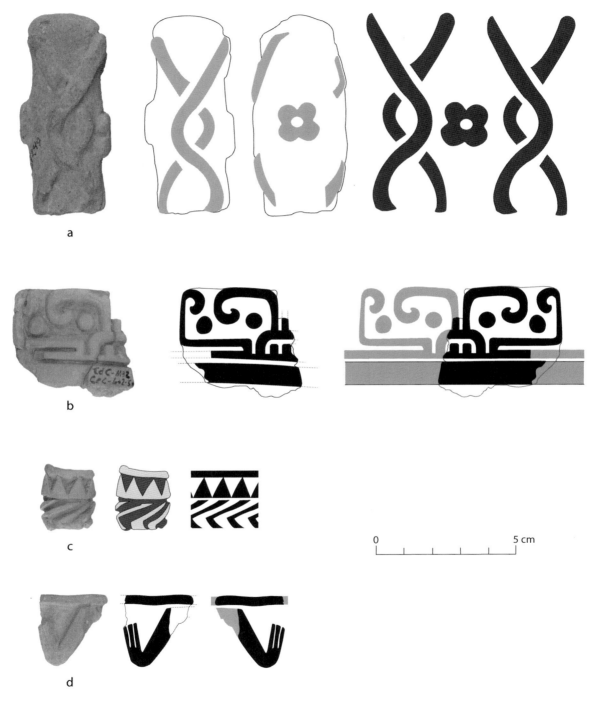

Figure A26. Cylindrical stamps, their designs (center) and impressions (right); a. semi-solid stamp (5249), b. hollow stamp with double merlon icon (5122); c. hollow stamp with geometric design of triangles and chevrons (5123-2); d. hollow stamp with arm and hand (5123-1). For the proposed impressions, black zones represent known elements of stamps, and gray elements are reconstructed portions.

Figure A27. Fragments of stemmed, flat stamps. a. raptorial bird (5124); b. geometric or iconic design (5125).

or floor of the stamp. This stamp was broken during excavation, and not all the pieces of it were recovered. The eye element is clearly evident in the floor of the stamp. Adding these and other elements, the half of design of the fragment appears to represent a raptorial bird with a sharp, downturned beak (Figure A27a). The stamp is 4.8 cm high from its face to the end

of its conical stem. The fragment is 5.7 cm long by 5.6 cm wide.

Geometric or iconic design (5125): This stamp follows the rectangular format. Judging from the preserved edges of the stamp and the slope of its back side, we have about 70 percent of the design. The top of the stem is missing. The design was probably about 6.5 cm long and

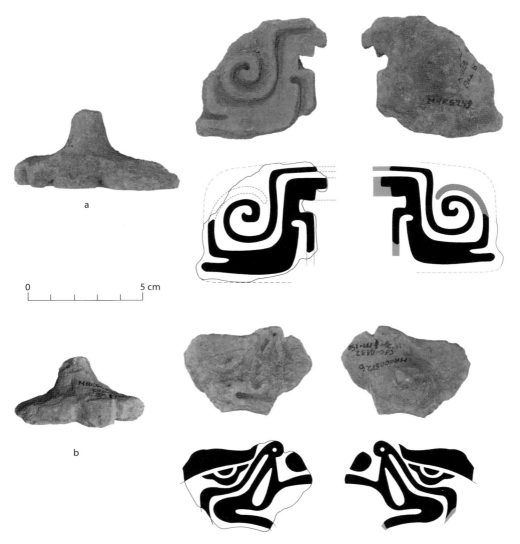

Figure A28. Fragments of stemmed, flat stamps; a. curvilinear design (5249-1), b. zoomorphic design, possibly a serpent head (5126).

3.5 cm wide and 3.5 cm from the flat face to the tip of the stem. It is made of fine tan paste (10YR 6/3 pale brown) and has a burnished surface. The design appears iconic or glyphic rather than purely geometric (Figure A27b). The fragment measures 3.3 by 5.3 cm in width and length, and it is 2.8 cm thick from the face to the end of its broken stem.

Curvilinear design (5249-1): This stamp appears to have a rectangular format, and its design has broad and bold curvilinear elements (Figure A28a). It is of medium-coarse paste and

deeply cut. It may be from an earlier era than the stamps just described. The stamp surface is smoothed but not burnished. The stamp is 3.4 cm high, 6.0 cm long, and 5.3 cm wide.

Zoomorphic design, possibly a serpent head (5126): This stamp appears to be made of the same paste as Stamp 5249-1, but is fired to a darker color (10YR 5/2 grayish brown) and is much more battered. Its design is hard to follow because much has been broken, and it was not as deeply cut, thus we cannot follow the clues on the floor of the stamp (Figure A28b). It appears

to be a zoomorphic design, perhaps of a serpent with an open mouth. It appears to be in a figure eight configuration. It is 3.2 cm thick at the stem. It is 5.7 cm long and 4.2 cm wide.

Rectangular stamp with complex design (5128-1): This stamp is the corner of a stamp of rectangular format. It is made of medium-coarse orange paste (5YR 6/4 light reddish brown) with a gray carbon core. It represents less than one-fourth of the original stamp. Its design shares basic elements with one published by Lee (1969: fig. 41b). The fragment is 4.0 cm long, 3.1 cm wide and 1.5 cm thick (Figure A29a).

Rectangular stamp with pyramid design (5128-4): This fragment may represent about a third of the original stamp. It is 3.0 cm long, 3.2 cm wide, and 1.0 cm thick. It is of reddish gray medium-fine paste (2.5YR 5/2 weak red) and has a polished and burnished printing surface. The stamp appears to have broken right under the stem. The design appears to be the "triangular form" described by Lee (1969: fig. 42) (Figure A27b). These stepped triangles may represent pyramids. This design is frequent enough at Chiapa de Corzo that one wonders whether it was a glyph that represented the site or its leaders.

Rectangular stamp with complex design (5128-3): This stamp is of very fine tan paste (5YR 6/4 light reddish brown) and has a deeply cut design through its flat, burnished surface. It appears to be a stamp of the irregular, figure eight format. The notched border is similar to that on stamp 5124, but it is not a fragment of this stamp (Figure A29c). This fragment is 3.7 cm long, 2.5 cm wide, and 1.8 cm thick. The lower slope of the broken stem is on the back of this stamp. It is well smoothed and burnished on its stemmed surface.

Rectangular stamp with complex design (5128-2): This stamp is made of very fine orange-red paste (7.5YR 6/4 light brown) and has smoothed surfaces, front and back. They may have been burnished, but the stamp is eroded. It is an edge fragment. There is no trace of a stem on the back side, so it was probably near one of the ends. It has triangular and curvilinear elements (Figure A29d). It is similar to a stamp illustrated by Lee (1969: fig. 44i). It is 3.6 cm long, 3.2 cm wide, and 1.3 cm thick.

Rectangular stamp depicting an animal head (5127): This flat stamp is made of fine, tan-to-brown paste (10YR 6/3 pale brown) and has a burnished surface. Unlike other stamps illustrated here, the stem of this stamp is askew. It is 3.7 cm thick from the tip of the stem to the face of the stamp. It appears to be of rectangular format, with the two ends missing. The flat face is 2.7 cm long and 2.5 cm wide. The design appears to be that of a rabbit or other long-eared mammal (Figure A30a).

Oval stamp of animal head (5129): This stamp is complete and only lacks a few elements of the design that have broken off. Even so, the design is not clear. It appears to be zoomorphic, perhaps a serpent with open mouth (Figure A30b). The stamp is 2.8 cm high at the stem, 3.6 cm long, and 2.8 cm wide. It is of medium-fine dark orange-brown paste (5YR 5/2 reddish gray) with temper. It has an irregular stamping surface, and some elements of the cut out design are more elevated than others. It would not have been an effective stamp for most media. It may have worked best on pliant and soft surfaces such as human flesh.

Circular stamp with swirl design (5130): The carved face of this stamp is complete and represents a swirl design (Figure A30c). The stem has been broken off the back. The stamp is 3.8 cm long, 3.6 cm wide, and 1.4 cm thick. It is of fine orange paste (10YR 6/3 pale brown) with fine temper.

Ornaments (Figure A31)

Bead (5132-1): This a subspherical bead with a hole with straight sides (Figure A31a). It is made of medium-fine orange paste. It is 1.5 cm tall and 1.6 cm in diameter. The hole is 5.0 mm in diameter.

Small tubular bead (5133-2): This bead is made of fine paste and slipped red. The fragment is 1.3 cm long and 6.3 mm in diameter (Figure A31b).

Long tubular bead (5133-1): This tubular bead is also made of fine paste. It is not slipped. It is 3.7 cm long and 7.7 mm in diameter. (Figure A31c)

Fragment of red eartube (5113-1): This is a fragment of a red-slipped eartube. It is 3.1 cm

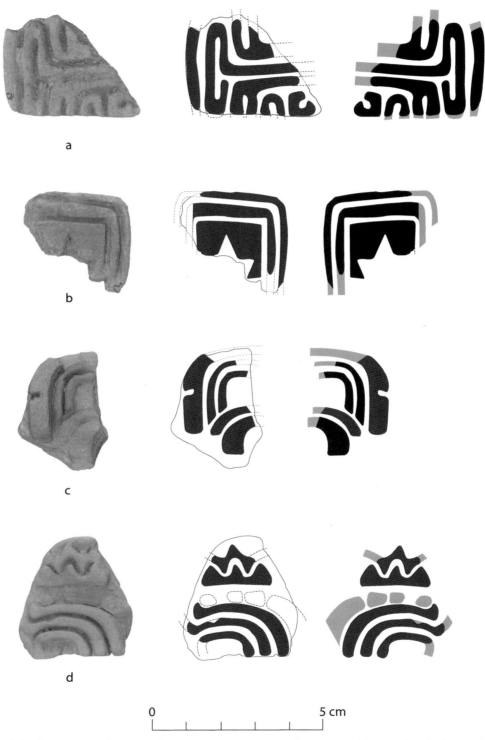

Figure A29. Fragments of stemmed, flat stamps; a. rectangular stamp with complex design (5128-1), b. rectangular stamp with pyramid design (5128-4), c. rectangular stamp with complex design (5128-3), d. rectangular stamp with complex design (5128-2).

Figure A30. Fragments of stemmed, flat stamps; a. rectangular stamp depicting an animal head (5127), b. oval stamp of animal head (5129), c. circular stamp with swirl design (5130).

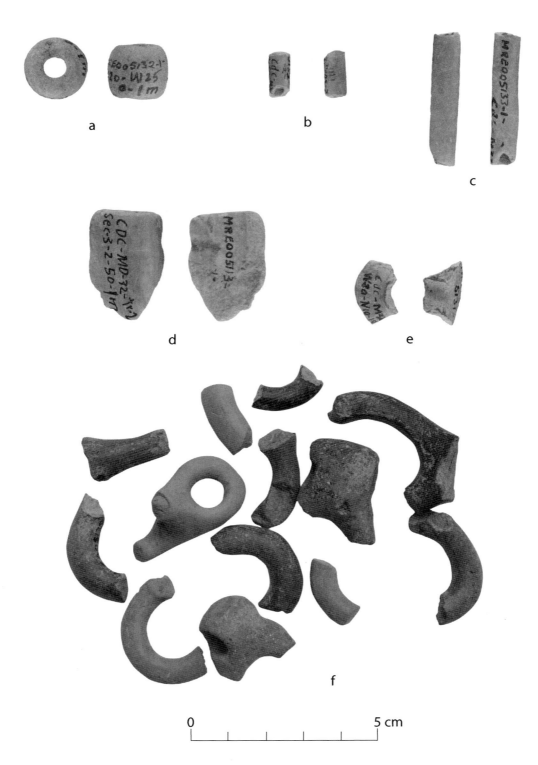

Figure A31. Miscellaneous ceramic artifacts; a. bead (5132-1), b. small tubular bead (5133-2), c. long tubular bead (5133-1), d. fragment of red eartube (5113-1), e. fragment of earspool (5131), f. fragments of double rings.

long and 1.9 cm wide (Figure A31d). It is made
of very fine paste.

Fragment of earspool (5131): This fragment
represents about one-fourth of the original
earspool made of fine, dark brown paste. It is
very thin, with walls and flares 4.1 mm thick
(Figure A31e). The original earspool would have
been 2.5 cm in diameter, with flares 9.5 mm
wide. The throat was 1.0 cm in diameter. The
throat is broken so we do no know the original
height of this ornament.

Double-Rings (Figure A31f)

Fragments of double rings: Thirteen
fragments of double-rings were found in the
Mound 32 excavations. Most are of fine paste
and burnished. Some are even slipped. Many
more fragments were found in the salvage
excavations of the nearby Mound 15. The double
rings from this mound were also larger and
thicker than those from Mound 32 (see Glauner
et al. 2017).

Sherd Disks (Figure A32)

Sherd disk lid fragment (5138-1): This disk
was made from the base of a red plate with fine,
orange-red paste. It is 9.0 cm in diameter and 5.5
mm thick (Figure A32a). It has a very carefully
shaped and ground edge. It was probably a lid
for a jar, such as found with Burial 297.

Irregular sherd disk (5138-2): This disk
is of coarse brown paste of a sherd from a
Middle Preclassic jar (Figure A32b). The disk is
irregular in outline and lacks dressed edges. It is
4.8 cm in diameter and 1.0 cm thick.

Irregular sherd disk (5138-4): This sherd
disk was made from a large fragment of a
polished red jar with fine orange paste. It has
irregular edges. It is 3.7 cm in diameter and 9.7
mm thick (Figure A32c).

Sherd disk with dressed edges (5138-3):
This disk was made from a base fragment of
a red bowl. It is of medium-fine paste. The
piece appears to have been well used, or have
been made from a pot that was. Most of the
slipped surface has been abraded off. It has a
very regular circular outline and well-formed,
dressed edges. It is 3.9 cm in diameter and 6.5
mm thick (Figure A32d).

Small sherd disk (5138-5): This tiny sherd
disk is similar to and of similar size to those
found at Mound 15 (Glauner et al. 2017). It
is made from a sherd from a thin red bowl.
Other than a counter for some game, we do not
know its function. As a lid, it would only be
appropriate for closing the spout of a spouted jar.
It is 1.5 cm in diameter and 5.1 mm thick (Figure
A32e).

Sandstone circular disk (5160): Technically,
this object does not belong in this category, but
it appears to be a functional equivalent of the
sherd disks. It is of hard, fine-grain, banded
yellow sandstone. It is dense and hard. Its edges
show chipping and grinding to bring it to its
current circular shape. It appears to have been
a lid. There is no evidence that the flat surfaces
were used to abrade other objects. It is 7.2 cm in
diameter and 1.4 cm thick (Figure A32f).

Sherd Abraders (Figure A32)

Sherd abrader (5139-1): This long,
rectangular sherd was made from a thick vessel
with medium-fine paste. This is an abrading tool
used in the hand in a sawing motion. It has four
grinding facets, two on each edge. The tool is
more worn in the middle of both edges. It is 6.2
cm long, 2.0 cm wide, and 1.8 cm thick (Figure
A32g).

Small sherd abrader (5139-2): This artifact
is a small version of the sherd abrading tool just
described. It is also made from a sherd with
medium-fine paste. It is 2.8 cm long and 1.1 cm
thick (Figure A32h). It also has two grinding
facets on each edge.

SHELL ARTIFACTS
Ornaments (Figure A33)

Olivella shell beads (5147): Eighteen olivella
shell beads were found (Figure A33a). They
must have been part of a necklace of some sort.
No such object is reported for the three burials,
but these beads must have come from a burial
or cache that is unreported. The longest of these
beads is 1.4 cm.

Shell disk (5140): This is another object that
likely came from a burial and was misplaced. It
is made from river clam shell. It has a very small
suspension hole at one edge (Figure A33b). The

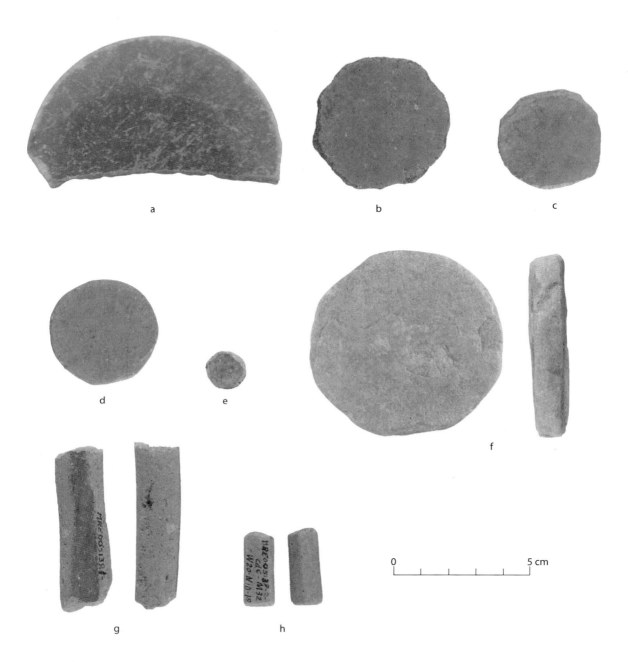

Figure A32. Worked sherds; a. sherd disk lid fragment (5138-1), b. irregular sherd disk (5138-2), c. irregular sherd disk (5138-4), d. sherd disk with dressed edges (5138-3), e. small sherd disk (5138-5); f. plan and profile views of sandstone circular disk (5160), g. front and back views of sherd abrader (5139-1), h. front and back views of small sherd abrader (5139-2).

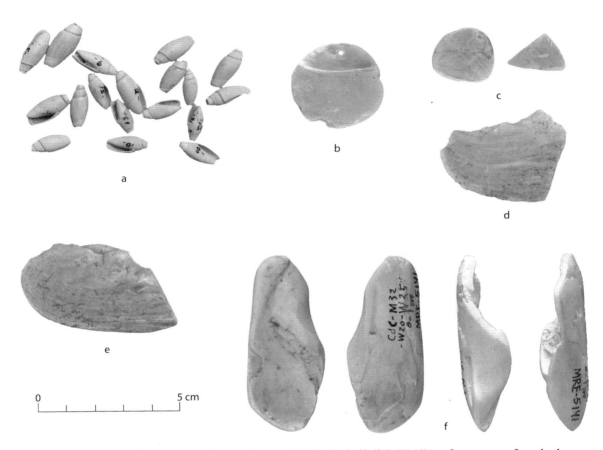

Figure A33. Shell artifacts; a. olivella shell beads (5147), b. shell disk (5140), c. fragments of worked shell (5142), d. cut clam shell (5144-11), e. cut clam shell (5144-10), f. front, back, and side views of a column of a conch shell, possibly a chisel (5141).

disk is 3.2 cm in diameter and 2.9 mm thick. It weighs 4.3 g.

Fragments of worked shell (5142): These two fragments of river clam shells have worked edges, but both lack suspension holes (Figure A33c). They could have been mosaic pieces or items that were still in the process of manufacture. The oval piece measures 2.1 by 2.0 cm, and the triangular piece is 1.8 by 1.4 cm.

Worked Shell (Figure A33)

Cut clam shell (5144-11): This a large segment of a river clam shell that has had one edge cut off at an angle (Figure A33d). It is 3.4 cm long and 4.4 cm wide.

Cut clam shell (5144-10): This cut clam shell is similar to that just described and exhibits

a transverse cut that removed its right edge (viewer's perspective) (Figure A33e). Both these cuts on the two clam shells are unusual but would be needed to make triangular pieces such as shown in Figure A33c. The cut clam shells found in the Mound 15 excavations were cut perpendicular to the line of the hinge of the shell. The objective was to cut out rectangular pieces with perpendicular sides (see Glauner et al. 2017). In addition to these two cut shells, another seven large fragments and 39 small fragments of clam shell were collected during the Mound 32 excavations. None of these, however, shows clear evidence of human modification and thus are not described or illustrated here. Nonetheless, it is worth noting that this is many more pieces of shell than found or saved during the Mound 15 excavations.

Column of a conch shell (5141):

This lozenge-shaped piece of shell is ground on all edges and both faces. At its thick, distal end, the shell column has been ground to produce a chisel-like edge, as evident in the two profiles of this piece shown in Figure A33f. Small chips have been broken from this edge, much like those that break from jade axes that have similar bits. There is no trace of pounding or bruising of the shell edge at the proximal of the piece, however. Therefore, if this shell object were used as a chisel, it must have been hafted in some fashion to avoid breaking or damaging the thin upper edge of the tool. Hafting this tool in a wooden haft would have allowed the worker to pound on the proximal end to use this shell tool as a chisel. It is 6.4 cm long, 2.7 cm wide, and 1.5 cm thick at its thickest part just above the bit. The shell is creamy white in color except where some layers of the outer portion of the shell have spalled off revealing a pinkish-purplish color. The exterior part of the tool (shown on the right in Figure A33f) was ground perpendicular to its long axis. The bit portion of the opposite face was ground perpendicular to the tool's long axis.

STONE ARTIFACTS

Limestone and Travertine Artifacts (Figure A34)

Carved travertine representing a human skull (5156): This thumb-size artifact is a small cylindrical piece of tan travertine with a bulbous end. A human skull has been carved in the wide end by making two broad cavities for eyes and a similar round cavity at each end of the mouth (Figure A34a). Four upper and six lower teeth are carved above and below an incised line for the tooth line. The back of the skull has been ground flat, and both sides of the upper skull have also been ground down, leaving a slight ridge on the top of the skull. The piece is 4.4 cm long, 1.9 cm wide at the nose, 2.1 cm thick at the same place, and weighs 19.7 g. The broken portion of the shaft has a cylindrical hole where the twig around which this rock coalesced used to be. The concentric growth rings of the rock are evident in this break. The stone is soft. This looks like a curious artifact and almost random

carving. In concept this piece is similar to a minor sculpture illustrated by Lee (1969: fig. 65) of a human head atop a small cylindrical piece of limestone.

Carved fragment of limestone (5155-2): This cylindrical piece of whitish gray limestone is broken off at both ends. It is roughly shaped and not smoothed. Numerous striations parallel to the long axis of the piece are evident. It is 4.1 cm long, 2.5 cm in diameter, and weighs 41.0 g (Figure A34b).

Carved limestone, probable hammer (5159): This piece of tan limestone shows evidence of work on all its surfaces. It is wedge-shaped in side view, has a squarish transverse cross-section at its wide end and tapers to thin edge at the other end (Figure A34c). A three-quarters groove has been ground near the tapered end. All faces show evidence of fine pecking and sculpting of this piece. Both of the ends, however, are rounded and battered, probably from the use of this tool as a hammer. In concept it looks rather similar to a ball-peen hammer, with one broad surface and a small rounded hammer at the other end. The object is 6.5 cm long, 3.3 cm wide at the broad end, 2.3 cm wide at the small end, and it weighs 78.0 g.

Double rim limestone eartube (5151): This artifact is a fragment of a well-made eartube of white to pinkish limestone. It has well-defined rims at both ends (Figure A34d). This fragment is about a fifth of the original ornament. It is 2.6 cm long and had an outside diameter of 2.2 cm. It is rather thick for this sort of ornament (3.2 mm wall thickness). It is well smoothed and polished on the outside surface. The pinkish cast of this stone may be from traces of red pigment. The breaks on this piece are ancient. It weighs 2.7 g; the original piece would have weighed about 12 g.

Incised, pierced limestone earplug (5149): This artifact type is described by Lee (1969:136), and he illustrates examples similar to this specimen. This pierced earplug is of yellowish white limestone. It is incised on one side, and the incision is covered with red pigment (Figure A34e). The earplug has constricted or concave sides. It is 1.7 cm long, 2.8 cm in diameter, and weighs 14.6 g. The central hole is 3.3 mm in diameter and has vertical sides. The deep rather

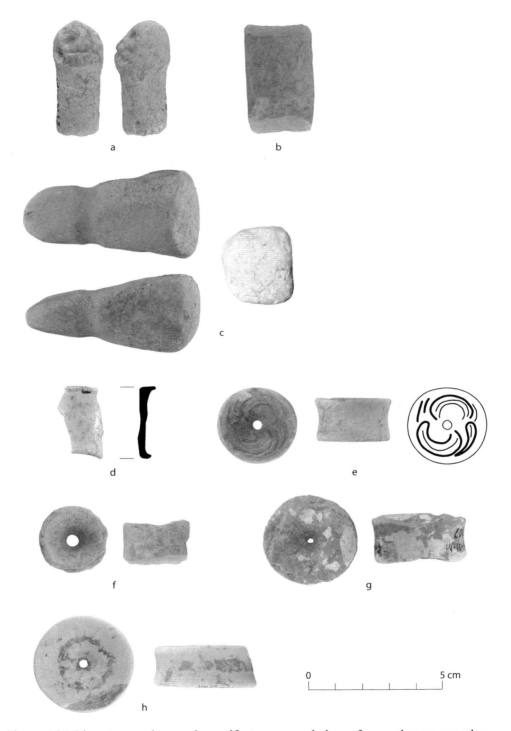

Figure A34. Limestone and travertine artifacts; a. carved piece of travertine representing a human skull (5156), b. carved fragment of limestone (5155-2), c. side and end views of a carved limestone, possibly used as a hammer (5159), d. fragment of a double rim travertine eartube (5151), e. plan and profile views of an incised limestone pierced earplug (5149); f. pierced limestone earplug (5150-3); g, pierced limestone earplug (5150-2), h. pierced limestone earplug (5150-1).

crudely incised design represents opposed arcs in mirror imagery (similar to one in Lee 1969: fig. 96j). It is not clear whether the current chalky white surface of this earplug (and the others) was created anciently or whether it is a consequence of some sort of weathering and hydration process. As evidence in some broken specimens, the white layer is very thin, and the inner core of these ornaments is gray. They may have been gray when originally made and used.

Pierced limestone earplug (5150-3): This small, pierced earplug is badly battered (Figure A34f). It is light gray in color, thus indicating that the white color of other earplugs may not be due to weathering since this earplug conserved its original color, and in obviously less-than-gentle circumstances. The white color may have been achieved by burning (we have not tested this idea). The outside throat of this piece is slightly constricted. The piece is 1.6 cm long, 2.5 cm in diameter, and weighs 12.2 g. It has an unusually large center hole 4.2 mm in diameter. This hole has been opened from biconical drilling sometime after the original earplug was made, as evident with the different inner planes of the ornament.

Pierced limestone earplug (5150-2): This pierced earplug of white limestone is also badly damaged on its outer edges and is encrusted with a layer of calcium carbonate (Figure A34g). It has a constricted, concave throat. It is 1.7 cm long or high, 3.4 cm in diameter, and weighs 20.6 g. The center hole is 1.7 mm in diameter, but this is covered with calcium that has closed the hole. It was probably about 3 mm in diameter like the pierced earplugs.

Pierced limestone earplug (5150-1): A large chip is missing from one face of this white limestone earplug (Figure A34h) and reveals its gray center as well as the thinness of the surface layer of white (1.0 mm thick). The outer throat of this pierced earplug is concave. It is 1.5 cm long, 3.7 cm in diameter, and weighs 24.1 g. There is no trace of incised design. The central perforation is 2.9 mm in diameter.

Metamorphic Stone Artifacts (Figure A35)

Brown stone axe (5158): This small axe or chisel is of unidentified dark brown stone. It is the only whole specimen found in the excavation. The chips from the rim are excavation damage (Figure A35a). The fact that it could suffer such damage from a shovel is evidence that the stone is not tough and would not have been suitable for heavy-duty work. The axe shows evidence of multiple resharpening and reshaping episodes. It has a squarish poll and is rectangular in transverse cross-section. It is 4.7 cm long, 2.4 cm wide, 1.1 cm thick, and weighs 25.4 g.

Fragment of greenstone axe (sn): This artifact is half the bit edge of a very large and thick axe of oval transverse cross-section (Figure A35b). The bit is still sharp and shows evidence of resharpening. The axe probably broke in use. It is of dark metamorphic stone but is not jade. The fragment is 4.7 cm long, 4.4 cm wide, 4.0 cm thick, and weighs 135.6 g.

Fragment of a greenstone axe (4860-5): This small piece is the corner from the bit of a greenstone axe with a rectangular transverse cross-section (Figure A35c). The stone is not jade but it is of that color. It is probably serpentine. It shows evidence of resharpening. Part of a chip from the edge was not totally obliterated in the resharpening. The axe had very crisp and well-defined margins. The fragment is 3.2 cm long, 2.2 cm wide, 1.5 cm thick, and weighs 12.8 g.

Axe fragment (5157): This fragment appears to include all of the bit of the massive axe from which it came. The axe broke in half, with the break initiating at one corner of the bit (Figure A35d). The stone appears to be dark volcanic stone with numerous white crystals. It was oval in transverse cross-section. The edge of the bit shows battering and blunting from use. This fragment is 5.7 cm long, 4.6 cm wide, 3.3 cm thick, and weighs 106.3 g.

Modified stone sphere (5162): This flattened sphere of dark brown stone evinces patches of grinding and smoothing and thus has been modified from its natural state. The modification, however, appears minor (Figure A35e). The stone is hard and dense, but we did not break it open to identify its class. It is 3.5 cm in diameter, 2.9 cm thick, and weighs 47.5 g.

Figure A35. Plan and profile views of lapidary stone artifacts; a. brown stone axe (5158), b. fragment of greenstone axe (sn), c. fragment of a jade axe (4860-5), d. axe fragment (5157), e. carved stone sphere (5162), f. sandstone reamer (5161), g. sandstone reamer (5155-1).

Sandstone Reamers (Figure A35)

Sandstone reamer (5161): This object is made of medium-fine yellow sandstone with strongly bonded grains. Other than a flake missing from one end, it is whole. All of its surfaces show evidence of rotary wear. Three different diameters and five different tapers are evident in its profile (Figure A35g). It is 10.1 cm long, 4.9 cm in maximum diameter, and weighs 270.0 g. It is by far the largest reamer known for Chiapa de Corzo (see Lee 1969: fig. 84).

Sandstone reamer (5155-1): This artifact is of medium grain reddish yellow sandstone. It is coarser grained and of looser bonding than Specimen 5161. This is just the tip of an abrader that may have been used as a reamer (Figure A35f). It is eroded and damaged, hence few traces of use-wear remain. It is squarish rather than round in transverse cross-section. It is 5.0 cm long, 2.4 cm wide, 2.1 cm thick, and weighs 36.8 g.

Groundstone Artifacts (Figures A36-A39)

Under the category of groundstone we include metates and manos. We have divided these according to the raw material used. Implements of basalt were imported from the farthest distance, perhaps highland Guatemala. The two manos of granite likely came from the Pacific coast of Chiapas near the area of Tonalá. Implements of dark, dense andesite may also have been imported from up river. Tools made of light andesite and sandstone were probably locally made within the immediate region of Chiapa de Corzo. Within each group, there appear to be manos of different design, but most of them were originally circular or nearly round in transverse cross-section and became transformed through extensive use into a variety of forms.

Basalt:

Metate (sn): Corner fragment of the distal end of a restricted metate, 11.0 cm long, 11.9 cm wide, 3.8 cm thick, 1280.1 g. The metate had well-carved sides that flared out slightly from the flat base to the upper grinding surface. The base is well smoothed from abrasion but not from grinding. One of the broken edges is rounded from use (Figure A36a).

Mano (sn): Medial fragment, circular transverse cross-section, some evidence of dogbone wear, 12.5 cm long, 8.0 cm in diameter, 1145.5 g. Both broken ends are rounded and battered from secondary use as a hammerstone. Traces of white cement adhere to its ends and part of its grinding surface, perhaps from use with making or applying cement (Figure A36b).

Mano (sn): End fragment, plano-convex in transverse cross-section but probably originally thick oval in section. One face of this well-worn mano has been used much more that the other, 15.8 cm long, 8.7 cm wide, 6.9 cm thick at its thicker end (the original middle of the mano) and 4.8 cm thick at the tapered end, 1158.5 g (Figure A36c).

Mano (sn): End fragment, thick oval transverse cross-section, mild dogbone wear on two faces, well-shaped end, 10.4 cm long, 7.3 cm wide, 5.7 cm thick on in used portion, 791.0 g (Figure A36d).

Mano (5235): Medial fragment, thick oval transverse cross-section, 8.2 cm long, 7.3 cm wide, 6.0 cm thick, 622.1 g. Evidence of dogbone wear. Thick end shows secondary use as a hammerstone. Not illustrated.

Dark Andesite:

Metate (5248): Proximal half of a slightly restricted basin metate 21.7 cm long, 23.7 cm wide, 3.2 cm thick at its most used portion (the original middle of the metate), 5.7 cm thick at the thick end, 4210.0 g. The original metate was probably about 50 cm long. Both lateral edges have been broken off, but there is no evidence of dogbone wear. The edges of the metate were well sculpted, with a expanding taper from the flat base to the upper face. The base is flat, with extensive sections of smoothed and polished surface, presumably from abrasion of using the metate on a flat surface. The upper face, or grinding surface, has numerous pock marks from resharpening, but the metate shows extensive use after the retooling of its surface (Figure A37a).

Mano (5218): End fragment, thick oval transverse cross-section, 132 cm long, 7.7 cm wide, 5.4 to 5.8 cm thick, 796.5 g. The preserved end shows rounding from use in a restricted metate rather than dogbone wear from a metate

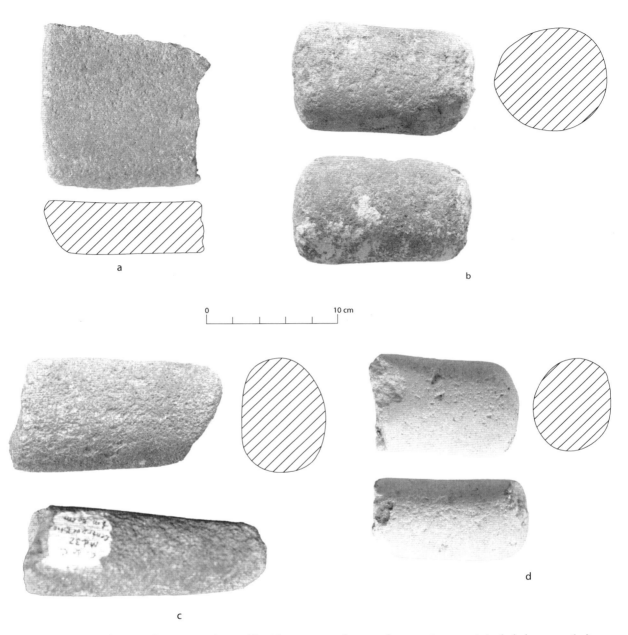

Figure A36. Views and cross-sections of basalt metate and mano fragments; a. metate (sn), b. mano (sn), c. mano (sn), d. mano (sn).

that was narrower than the mano was long. Both ends show battering from secondary use as a hammerstone after the mano broke. There are pecked margins between its two smoothed faces, perhaps the texture of the original metate (Figure A37b).

Mano (5228): End fragment of a mano with four grinding facets; it was probably an oval

mano originally. It has a very well-dressed end from fine pecking (Figure A37c). It is 13.2 cm long, 7.6 cm wide at its widest part and 4.6 to 5.8 cm thick, 753.4 g. This fragment probably is at least half of the original mano, which would have been about 25 cm long. There are traces of red pigment in the pores of two adjoining grinding facets from grinding red mineral.

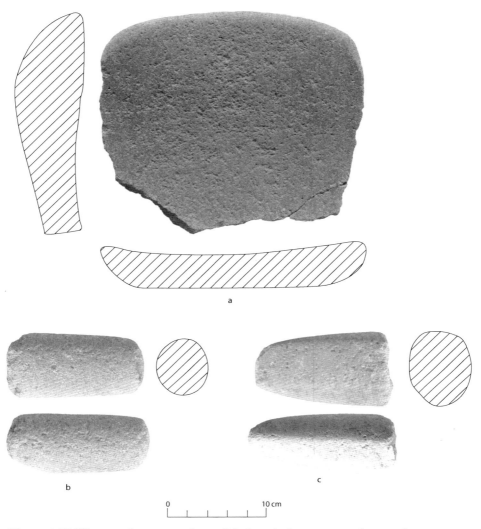

Figure A37. Views and cross-sections of dark andesite metate and mano fragments; a. metate (5248), b. Mano (5218), c. mano (5228).

Mano (5231): End fragment, plano convex in transverse cross-section but probably originally circular, 9.2 cm long, 7.9 cm wide, 4.9 to 5.9 cm thick, 638.9 g. The preserved end is beveled. If the other end was its mirror image, the mano would have been trapezoidal in side view. This means that the two grinding surfaces would have been a significantly different lengths. This could have been a design feature of the mano, allowing its use in metates of different widths. The original pitting from fabrication is evident in the margins between the opposing grinding faces (Figure A38a).

Mano (5222): End fragment, circular transverse cross-section, extreme dogbone wear on one face, 8.3 cm long, 6.5 cm wide, 5.0 cm thick at the end, 3.5 cm thick in the worn section, 376.9 g. The margins between the two grinding faces still show pockmarks from manufacture (Figure A38b).

Mano (5225): End fragment, circular transverse cross-section, significant dogbone wear on all grinding surfaces, 6.2 cm long, 6.3 cm in diameter at unworn end, 5.5 cm diameter in the most worn part, 309.0 g. The unworn end indicates that this mano was always used on a

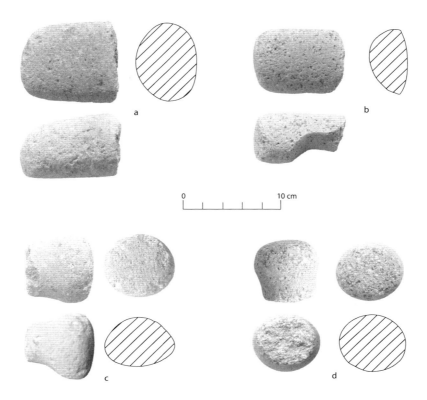

Figure A38. Views and cross-sections of dark andesite metate and mano fragments; a. mano (5231), b. mano (5222), c. mano (5225), d. mano (5224).

metate that was more narrow than the mano was long, thus the mano ends extended beyond the edges of the metate and resulted in significant dogbone wear (Figure A38c).

Mano (5224): End fragment, originally circular transverse cross-section, significant dogbone wear on all grinding faces, 6.3 cm long, 6.3 cm wide, 5.8 cm thick, 336.7 g (Figure A38d).

Mano (5226): End fragment, thin oval transverse cross-section, 8.9 cm long, 7.6 cm wide, 5.6 cm thick, 547.4 g. This mano has very smooth grinding surfaces, one of which has evidence of dogbone wear. The original end shows minor evidence of pounding from use as a hammer. Not illustrated.

Mano (5229): End fragment, lenticular transverse cross-section, 8.9 cm long, 8.5 cm long, 4.8 cm thick, 573.0 g. Not illustrated.

Mano (5233): End fragment, thin oval transverse cross-section, 7.7 cm long, 6.8 cm wide, 5.9 cm thick, 466.5 g. The original end of the mano shows secondary use as a hammerstone. Not illustrated.

Light Andesite:

Metate (sn): Corner fragment of the distal end of a restricted metate with curved edges, 12.9 cm long, 7.5 cm wide, 4.7 cm thick at its thick end (original middle of metate), 634.5 g. Tapered edge from top to a narrower base. The base shows patches of smoothing from abrasion from being moved frequently on a flat surface (Figure A39a).

Mano (5238): Medial fragment of a mano of lenticular transverse cross-section, 9.0 cm long, 9.8 cm wide, and 4.7 cm thick. The margins between the two very smooth grinding surfaces show pecking marks—perhaps part of the original dressed surface from manufacture. Both ends are battered, but not from secondary use as a hammerstone (Figure A39b).

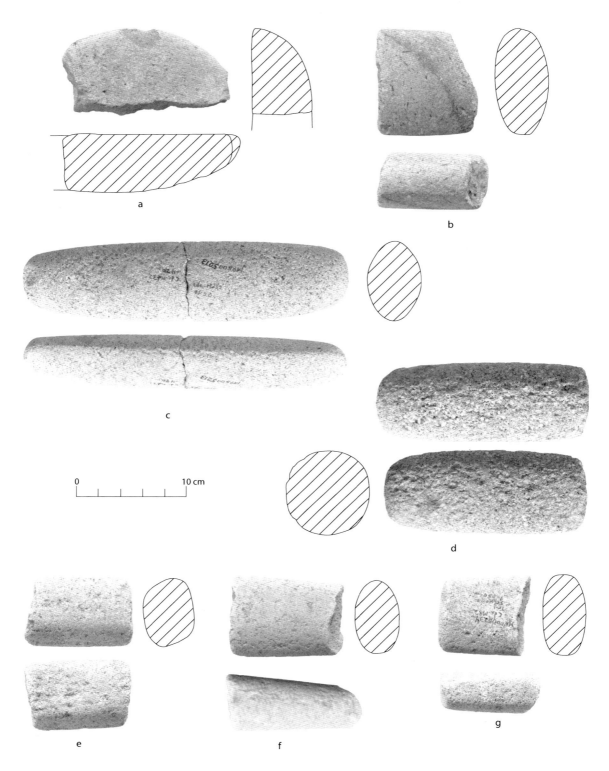

Figure A39. Views and cross-sections of light andesite metate and mano fragments; a. metate (sn), b. mano (5238), c. mano (5213), d. mano (5215), e. mano (sn), f. mano (sn), g. mano (5234).

Mano (5213): This is the only complete mano found in the Mound 32 excavations. It is broken, but not obviously from excavation. The break is probably an old one. This mano has an elliptical transverse cross-section and is 28.1 cm long, 4.6 cm wide, 4.7 cm thick; it weighs 1290.6 g. The very ends of this mano curve up, indicating it was used in a restricted metate that had to have been at least 30 cm wide. One surface is more curved than the other and was probably the grinding face that was favored in the later life of the mano. This surface shows fresh pecking marks that may indicate that this mano broke in the process of resharpening its slick grinding faces (Figure A39c).

Mano (5215): End fragment of a nearly whole mano with circular transverse cross-section, 17.2 cm long, 7.6 cm wide, 7.0 cm thick, 1406.0 g. This is the most interesting mano found in the excavations. All of its surfaces show deep pock marks from pecking and no smoothed facets from grinding. This looks like a mano that broke during manufacture. The depth of the pits indicate a very hard and sharp stone pick was used in manufacture. The broken end of this mano is worked like the other, but it is clearly broken, as evident in the asymmetry of the mano viewed in long cross-section (Figure A39d).

Mano (sn): Medial section of a mano originally of oval transverse cross-section, 8.9 cm long, 6.4 cm wide, 4.9 cm thick, 464.0 g. This fragment is interesting because it has four different grinding facets and has developed a rhomboid cross section (Figure A39e).

Mano (sn): Medial fragment of a mano of elliptical transverse cross-section, 10.2 cm long, 7.3 cm wide, 4.4 cm thick, 495.6 g (Figure A39f).

Mano (5234): End fragment of mano lenticular in transverse cross-section, 7.8 cm long, 7.1 cm wide, 3.7 cm thick, 354.9 g. The margins between the grinding faces are pecked and not smoothed from use. The end is battered, but not from secondary use as a hammerstone (Figure A39g).

Mano (5223): End fragment, circular transverse cross-section, pronounced dogbone wear on two faces, 7.9 cm long, unworn end 6.4 cm in diameter, 424.5 g. Not illustrated.

Mano (sn): Medial section, circular transverse cross-section, all faces are smoothed, 5.8 cm long, 7.0 cm in diameter at thick end, 6.6 cm in diameter at narrower end, 416.2 g. The narrow end shows secondary use as a hammerstone. Not illustrated.

Sandstone:

Metate (5246): Corner of the proximal half of a metate of coarse-grain, yellow-gray sandstone with moderately cemented grains, 20.1 cm long, 13.5 cm wide, 3.0 cm thick at most used middle section, 61.6 cm thick near the original end, 2740.0 g. It has a rough surface from resharpening. The lateral margins of this metate are rounded downward, indicating that a dogbone mano was used on this metate. The photograph shows three large divots in the surface of this implement (Figure A40a); these are excavation damage and not original.

Bench Fragment (5244): This is a medial fragment of an object of unknown size. The long slab leg on the underside of this piece is reminiscent of legs of Late Classic metates. But the wear on the upper face of this piece is from manufacture. The surface is flat but uneven, and it shows no traces of grinding wear. It looks like a fragment of a small bench. It is of coarse, reddish yellow sandstone with loosely cemented grains. It sheds its grains easily. It is 8.7 cm long, 9.0 cm wide, 8.6 cm wide on the flat part, 493.8 g (Figure A40b).

Mano (5227): End fragment of yellow sandstone with bands of fine pebble conglomerate; thin oval cross-section, 14.3 cm long, 8.9 cm wide, 6.0 cm thick, 1296.0 g. One grinding face is of fine-grain sandstone, and the other is of fine pebble conglomerate or very coarse sandstone. The tops of the pebbles are sheared off from grinding. The fine-grind face shows slight dogbone wear at its end (Figure A40c).

Mano (5220): Fine-grain yellow sandstone end fragment of mano with original oval or circular transverse cross-section; 13.5 cm long, 6.7 cm wide, 3.5 cm thick in most used portion, 6.3 cm thick at unused end, 773.3 g. In side view its upper surface is straight. It is very smooth. The face with significant dogbone wear is pecked from resharpening. It is likely that the

Figure A40. Views and cross-sections of sandstone metate and mano fragments; a. metate (5246), b. mano (5244), c. mano (5227), d. mano (5220), e. mano (5236), f. mano (5232), g. mano (5237).

attempt to resharpen this surface broke the tool because there is no evidence that any of these marks have been ground from subsequent use. The dogbone wear on this mano is typical of those that show it. The unused ends extended only about 3 to 4 cm beyond the margins of the metate. The regularity in the lengths of the unworn portions indicate standardization in the sizes of both manos and metates (Figure A40d).

Mano (5232): Fine-grain, yellow sandstone end fragment of a thin oval mano; 9.7 cm long, 6.8 cm wide, 5.1 cm thick, 624.6 g (Figure A40f).

Mano (sn): Yellowish sandstone with loose, coarse grain, medial fragment, thick oval transverse cross-section, 8.2 cm long, 6.3 cm wide, 5.6 cm thick, 437.4 g, battered end and cracked. Not illustrated.

Obdurate Sandstone:

Mano (5236): Yellow-gray, obdurate sandstone medial fragment of a triangular cross-section mano, probably originally oval in cross-section; 4.2 cm long, 5.6 cm wide, 5.0 cm thick, 227.6 g. All three facets are very smooth (Figure A40e).

Mano (5237): Red obdurate sandstone mano end fragment of triangular transverse cross-section, 6.2 cm long, 6.0 cm wide, 4.7 cm thick, 326.8 g (Figure A40g).

Mano (sn): Light gray obdurate sandstone, medial fragment, thick oval transverse cross-section, 10.4 cm long, 6.3 cm wide, 5.7 cm thick, 403.0 g. Not illustrated.

Mano (5217): Red obdurate sandstone, end fragment, lenticular cross-section, 13.7 cm long, 6.7 cm wide, 4.3 cm thick, 729.8 g. Not illustrated.

Granite:

Mano (5216): Fragment of a nearly complete mano of white granite; 18.9 cm long, 7.8 cm wide, 5.7 cm thick, 1458.3 g. The mano was thick oval to circular in original transverse cross-section and had two tapered edges, which gave it a trapezoidal shape in side view. It has three worn faces that have resulted in a triangular, transverse cross-section. The three faces are covered with red pigment, but none is on the ends or the crest between the two short faces. It was used to grind this pigment (Figure A41d).

Mano (5221): End fragment of pinkish granite of thick oval transverse cross-section that shows dogbone wear on one face; 8.8 cm long, 7.7 cm wide, 5.8 cm thick, 714.4 g. The surfaces are all highly polished from use; there is no evidence of secondary use as a hammerstone. Not illustrated.

Abrading Stones (Figure A40)

Sandstone boulder (5245): Fine-grain yellow sandstone with one concave surface from abrasion; 19.5 cm long, 17.3 cm wide, 6.3 cm thick, 2580.0 g. Most of this stone is discolored red from burning. The concavity from use as a stationary abrading stone is confined to one surface; the undersurface is flat but irregular. The abraded surface shows two different curves in transverse cross-section, indicating an early use as a flatter surface cut through by the more concave surface. In longitudinal cross-section the grinding surface is flat (Figure A41a).

Sandstone block (5243): Hard, fine-grain, yellow sandstone with fine banding with one naturally straight side and two edges chipped to form a rectangular form in plan view; 17.4 cm long, 13.4 cm wide, 5.0 cm thick, 2419.6 g. One surface is covered with red pigment as if ground on this surface, but there is no clear evidence of abrasion by a handstone. The pigment could have been applied to the surface rather than ground on it. The stone appears to be a building stone used in a wall rather than a tool (Figure A41b).

Pebble conglomerate abrader (5214): Cobble of coarse-grain pebble conglomerate that has been shaped on all surfaces; 19.3 cm long, 10.3 cm wide at widest point, 5.4 cm thick, 2035.2 g. The upper surface is slightly concave from use, probably as an abrader for rather soft materials. None of the pebbles have been sheared as occurs with manos used on metates. This was probably an abrader used in the hand rather than a stationary tool against which other objects were abraded (Figure A41c).

Figure A41. Views and cross-sections of miscellaneous groundstone artifacts; a. sandstone abrading stone (5245), b. sandstone block (5243), c. pebble conglomerate abrader (5214), d. granite mano (5216), e. granite mano (5221).

Sculpted Stone:

Andesite hemisphere (5242): This cobble looks like a giant handstone or a handstone for two hands; 16.0 cm long, 15.3 cm wide, 10.5 cm thick, 3590.0 g. Its flattish face is convex and evinces traces of polish. Its domed surface is carefully shaped as are its sides. A recessed margin from one to two centimeters wide is evident at the juncture between the flattish and domed surfaces. This band has been pecked. It appears that the stone was being shaped into an object that was never finished (Figure A42a).

Figure A42. Views of miscellaneous stone artifacts; a. andesite hemisphere (5242), b. spherical hammerstone (sn), c. quartzite sculpting hammerstone (5241), c. quartzite hammerstone (5240), e. andesite handstone (5239).

Hammerstone and Handstones (Figure A42)

Spherical hammerstone (sn): Reddish gray stone of obdurate sandstone or quartzite used as a hammerstone or a purposely manufactured stone sphere; 5.8 cm in diameter, 5.3 cm high,

270.0 g. The stone is very dense. It looks like a finishing hammer for sculpting work rather than a tool for knapping other stone. Its more flat surfaces are well shaped but show no evidence as having been used for grinding (Figure A42b).

Quartzite sculpting hammerstone (5241): Roundish black quartzite cobble used as a hammerstone-pick to sculpt groundstone tools; 8.5 cm long, 8.3 cm wide, 7.4 cm thick, 810.0 g. This tools shows extensive wear, especially on ridges left by removing flakes from its ends. This is a classic example of a hammer used to sculpt other stone (Figure A42c).

Quartzite hammerstone (5240): Oval cobble of quartzite with yellowish cortex; 10.0 cm long, 7.0 cm wide, 5.5 cm thick, 546.3 g. The pointed nose of this cobble was used as a hammerstone without any modification. The wear is slight. It would have been a good hammerstone-pick for using to shape groundstone (Figure A42d).

Andesite handstone (5239): Small, spherical cobble that shows a patch of polish on its more curved surface; 8.1 cm in diameter, 8.1 cm wide, 6.5 cm thick, 490.0 g. This stone shows some battering on its sides and may have seen minor service as a hammerstone as well as a handstone for minor grinding (Figure A42e).

Chipped Obsidian Artifacts (Figures A43 and A44)

We treat the numerous pieces of obsidian from the Mound 32 excavations in bulk rather than individually. All of the pieces come from two sources located in highland Guatemala: El Chayal and San Martín Jilotepeque (SMJ). The SMJ source is a day or two foot travel closer to Chiapa de Corzo than the El Chayal source. All of the obsidian artifacts relate to the blade industry. Almost all of the artifacts are fragments of fine pressure blades, which we present in Figures A43 and A44 by the type of fragment of the blades: proximal, medial, or distal. No exhausted blade cores, or fragments of them, were found in the Mound 32 excavations, and this is unusual. The illustrations also show bipolar flakes made on sections of thick blades or fragments of macroblades (made by percussion instead of pressure). The low frequency of pieces of percussion blades is also surprising because they were a popular product imported into Chiapa de Corzo in Middle Preclassic times. Given the number of early figurine fragments found at Mound 32 in the general fill, our expectation is that fragments of

earlier blades should have been part of the mix of earlier materials, as they were at Mound 15 (see Glauner et al. 2017).

The virtual absence of macroblade fragments in the materials from Mound 32 suggest that the age range represented by the artifacts from this mound is more restricted than the obsidian artifacts found at Mound 15, and hence, a better indicator of the nature of the obsidian trade during Guanacaste times. If so, it would indicate that most of the obsidian came from the El Chayal source, and much of it was imported as finished blades (see Clark and Lee 2007). Evidence in support of this supposition is the presence of very wide blades of this material, some of them possibly small percussion blades (Figure A43b). But the presence of first-series flakes (Figure A43a) is clear evidence that much of the obsidian was imported as cores ready for pressure flaking. The range of widths of the blades (Figure A43b-d) is also evidence of local manufacture of many of these at Chiapa de Corzo. The absence of any manufacturing debris in the Mound 32 materials indicates that these blades were not made at this location.

Much of what was mentioned for the blade-related obsidian artifacts of El Chayal obsidian also applies to those from the SMJ source. There are fewer artifacts of this material, and the near absence of distal blade fragments is surprising (Figure A43e). A few of these blades could be Middle Preclassic artifacts that came in with the fill. One-hundred and forty-one pieces of obsidian were found and individually recorded in the Mound 32 excavations, of which 99 (70.2 %) are of El Chayal obsidian and 42 (28.2 %) are of SMJ obsidian. By weight, El Chayal obsidian constitutes 68.3 percent (241.0 g.) and SMJ obsidian 31.7 percent (112.0 g.) of the total.

Almost all the obsidian blade fragments show clear evidence of use on both their edges for a range of cutting tasks, presumably mostly domestic. Not surprisingly, the widest and thickest blades were used for the most heavy duty tasks (cutting hard and very hard materials), and the narrower blades were used for lighter work (cutting medium and soft materials). What is surprising is that almost no

Figure A43. Flakes and blades of El Chayal obsidian; a. first-series flakes, b. proximal fragments of wide blades, c. proximal fragments of normal blades, d. medial fragments of pressure blades, e. distal fragments of pressure blades.

Figure A44. Flakes and blades of El Chayal and San Martín Jilotepeque (SMJ) obsidian; a. bipolar flakes made on El Chayal blade fragments, b. bipolar flakes made on SMJ blade fragments, c. proximal fragments of SMJ blades, d. medial fragments of SMJ pressure blades, e. distal fragments of SMJ blades.

blade edges were used for scraping (4.0 %), and only 5.0 percent of blade edges lack macroscopic evidence of use. There is no clear evidence of specialized use of obsidian tools at this mound. The presence of bipolar flakes on thick pieces of obsidian indicates some recycling of old materials, but this is infrequent compared to that known for Protoclassic sites. There is no clear evidence that obsidian artifacts were scarce at Mound 32, used to exhaustion, or extensively recycled.

REFERENCES CITED

AGRINIER, PIERRE
2000   *Mound 27 and the Middle Preclassic Period at Mirador, Chiapas, Mexico.* Papers of the New World Archaeological Foundation, No. 58. Brigham Young University, Provo.

CLARK, JOHN E.
2017   Mound 15 Caches and Burials in Site Perspective. In *The Archaeological Salvage of Mound 15, Chiapa de Corzo, Chiapas, Mexico*, by Darlene Glauner, Suzanne Herman, and John E. Clark, pp. 259-294. Papers of the New World Archaeological Foundation, No. 81. Brigham Young University, Provo.

CLARK, JOHN E., AND THOMAS A. LEE, JR.
2007   The Changing Role of Obsidian Exchange in Central Chiapas. In *Archaeology, Art, and Ethnogenesis in Mesoamerican Prehistory: Papers in Honor of Gareth W. Lowe*, edited by Lynneth S. Lowe and Mary E. Pye, pp. 109-159. Papers of the New World Archaeological Foundation, No. 68. Brigham Young University, Provo.

GLAUNER, DARLENE, AND SUZANNE HERMAN
1972   Archaeological Salvage at Mound 15, Chiapa de Corzo, Chiapas, Mexico. Paper presented at the 37th Annual Meetings of the Society for American Archaeology, Miami Beach, May.

GLAUNER, DARLENE, SUZANNE HERMAN, AND JOHN E. CLARK
2017   *The Archaeological Salvage of Mound 15, Chiapa de Corzo, Chiapas, Mexico.* Papers of the New World Archaeological Foundation, No. 81. Brigham Young University, Provo.

LEE, THOMAS A.
1969   *The Artifacts of Chiapa de Corzo, Chiapas, Mexico.* Papers of the New World Archaeological Foundation, No. 26, Brigham Young University, Provo.

LOWE, GARETH W.
1962   *Mound 5 and Minor Excavations, Chiapa de Corzo, Chiapas, Mexico.* Papers of the New World Archaeological Foundation, No. 12. Brigham Young University, Provo.

1995   Presencia maya en la cerámica del Preclásico Tardío en Chiapa de Corzo. In *Memorias del Segundo Congreso Internacional de Mayistas*, pp. 321-341. UNAM, Mexico.

LOWE, GARETH W., AND PIERRE AGRINIER
1960   *Mound 1, Chiapa de Corzo, Chiapas, Mexico.* Papers of the New World Archaeological Foundation, No. 8. Brigham Young University, Provo.

MILLER, DON E.
2014   *Excavations at La Libertad, A Middle Formative Ceremonial Center in Chiapas, Mexico.* Papers of the New World Archaeological Foundation, No. 64. Brigham Young University, Provo.

NAVARRETE, CARLOS
1978   La etapa postolmeca en Chiapas y Guatemala, *Historia de México*, Vol. II. pp. 297-307, Salvat Editores, Mexico.

PETERSON, FREDERICK
1963   *Some Ceramics from Mirador, Chiapas.* Papers of the New World Archaeological Foundation, No. 15. Brigham Young University, Provo.